THE DISCUSSION

A Practical Guide to the Theory Requirements
of the LAMDA Speech and Drama Examinations

by Carol Schroder, LLAM

with biographical material by
Valerie King LLAM (Hons), LGSM, Cert.Ed.

OBERON BOOKS
LONDON

ISBN 1 870259 71 8

Cover design: Andrzej Klimowski

Cover typography: Richard Doust

CONTENTS

CONTENTS

Introduction, Page 5

INTRODUCTION

This book aims to prepare candidates for the discussion part of the LAMDA examinations in The Speaking of Verse and Prose. The basic syllabus requirements for each grade are listed[1], alongside details of the qualities examiners are looking for in prospective candidates. This book will also examine the theoretical requirements of the examinations, and provide definitions of speech theory. **These definitions are a general guide, for reference purposes only**. Obviously, individual teachers will have their own approach to the subject.

Candidates are often convinced that the discussion with the examiner will be both a taxing and frightening experience. They are also worried by the whole idea of learning what is reverentially referred to as "the theory". In reality, the theoretical side of the examination should not prove a major stumbling block, especially if it has been introduced at an early stage into the candidate's scheme of learning.

The examinations are specifically designed to ease candidates through the more detailed aspects of theory. Thus, the examinations operate as a series, establishing a body of knowledge which is expanded from grade to grade. Candidates should understand that there are no hidden traps or surprises, and that the theoretical information required is highly approachable.

It is also important to remember that theory and performance **co-exist**. One illuminates the other.

Theory must always have a **practical application**. Theory is always more easily understood when applied directly to the candidate's practical work. In this way, theory takes on a specific and personal relevance, and avoids becoming academic.

In turn, the candidate's performance will benefit, as theory provides the background and support to the practical work. Practical use of theoretical information will lead to a greater understanding of the text, and the different ways in which the text can be approached and performed.

THEORY AND PRACTICE MUST ALWAYS BE INTER-RELATED.

[1] 1st September 1996 - 31st August 2000 edition

PART ONE

THE DISCUSSION

THE EXAMINER'S APPROACH

points to remember

* Examiners do not have a 'hidden agenda.' All questions will relate to the material used by the candidate and the specific syllabus requirements for each grade.

* Candidates will find that, more often than not, it is their *own* work which prompts the questions.

* Examiners will ask practical questions. In response, the candidate entering grade examinations should *demonstrate* rather than define. In the medal examinations definitions will be more necessary.

* Obviously, not all aspects of the syllabus can be covered within the prescribed time-limit.

* Questions relating to previous grades may be asked, at any stage.

* Examiners may discuss any relevant weaknesses shown in the candidate's practical work.

* Examiners will not usually contradict ideas unless they are patently inaccurate.

GRADE 1 - GRADE 3

In the syllabus there is no specific mention of the discussion. However, the examiner will invariably make conversation with the candidate.

This will take the form of a simple, personal (rather than theoretical) discussion. The examiner is interested in the candidate as a person, and will encourage him/her to contribute to the conversation. This will ensure that candidates are not afraid to air their views when the time comes for them to do so.

Basic questions might be asked on the poems chosen, the reasons for choice, and (sometimes) the meaning of individual words. Candidates should take note of the contrasts in mood and feeling between the poems. They should also be able to tell the examiner why they made that particular selection. However, it is important to remember that such an informal discussion will not be marked by the Examiner.

These early grades are very important - they set the tone for any further examinations entered. Therefore, the examiner will try to make candidates feel relaxed, and introduce them to an examination environment conducive to the best possible performance.

GRADE 4

There are no marks given for discussion until this grade.

SYLLABUS

The candidate will discuss the content of the selections with the examiner. The whole book from which the prose selection is taken must have been read and may be discussed. The meaning of individual words in both selections must be understood. A general understanding of the mood, style and content of both selections is expected.

In this grade, candidates are required to display a general understanding of their poetry and prose selections:

* what is the mood and style of the poem? (a simple response will suffice, for instance, is it happy or sad?)

* when was the book written? (i.e. is it a classic, or is it a contemporary/modern work?)

* what style is it written in? (a simple response will be satisfactory)

* how can this style be communicated to the listener? (e.g. characterisation, methods of introducing dialogue, the use of pause, the use of vocal flexibility)

* how does the extract relate to the overall storyline of the book?

* where does it fit in?

* what is the extract's importance to the rest of the book?

* who are the characters in the extract? What kind of people are they?

* what kind of language is the book written in? (again, only simple responses are necessary - modern/old-fashioned, formal/colloquial, conversational etc.)

IF THE BOOK FROM WHICH THE SELECTION HAS BEEN EXTRACTED IS UNAVAILABLE, A DIFFERENT SELECTION SHOULD BE CHOSEN[2]

The teacher should always encourage the candidate to embark on some contextual, background reading. This will broaden the candidate's knowledge.

GRADE 5

SYLLABUS

The candidate will discuss the content of the selections with the examiner. The whole book from which the prose selection is taken must have been read and may be discussed. An understanding of the mood, style and content of both selections is expected. In addition, the

[2] Please consult general notes on Page 15 of the syllabus

candidate may be required to appreciate the difference in form between a poem and a piece of prose.

DEFINITIONS[3]

POETRY is the artistic expression of the human mind in emotional and rhythmical language.

VERSE is a metrical line in accordance with the recognised rules of prosody. Verse has versification (or **metre**) and sometimes **rhyme**.

METRE is the pattern of poetry, determined by the number of heavy and light beats in a line.

RHYTHM is the musical flow of a poem or prose.

PROSE is the ordinary form of the written or spoken language, consisting of units or words forming sentences, paragraphs etc.

PROSE HAS RHYTHM. VERSE HAS RHYTHM AND METRE (OR IN MODERN VERSE - SHAPE)

A poem has different rhythmical and metrical qualities to prose. This difference in form should be apparent when speaking one or other.

At this level, candidates should also start becoming aware of the theoretical basics. For instance, the use of technical pause in speech as it directly affects the performance of their selections[4].

Knowledge of these will help bring out the meaning of the text, and maintain the structure of the poem or verse.

GRADE 6

SYLLABUS

The candidate will discuss with the examiner any aspect of theory already specified for previous grades. The whole book from which the

---

[3] Based around definitions from *The Concise Oxford Dictionary* (8th edition, Oxford University Press)

[4] For further details consult the information listed for the Grade 8 examination

prose selection is taken must have been read and may be discussed. The examiner will also expect the candidate to show a simple understanding of breathing and speaking, the muscles involved, and how and where the breath is changed into sound and, subsequently, speech. The candidate may be asked to demonstrate.

The essential word here is **understanding**. It is not enough for candidates to recite by rote the theoretical information required. Again, they must be aware of the practical application of theory. Hence, they might be required to actually **demonstrate** their knowledge of the subject.

Candidates will not need an extensive knowledge of biological terms, as questions on breathing will be simple. Very few technical terms will be required.

The candidate must, however, know the **location** of the breathing organs, and be able to point to the position of the diaphragm, the voice-box (larynx) etc.

The candidate must also understand the function of these organs and how they work.

BREATHING

Breathing and voice production is a wide-ranging and complicated subject, and a field where many experts disagree. The following analysis of breathing and voice production is a simple summary of the information needed to approach the subject *at this level.*

It is important to breathe in the correct way, so that you have enough breath to sustain your voice. This will enable you to speak a phrase easily in one breath. It is vital that your voice is relaxed in order that you can project.

Breathing for speech is conscious and controlled. **Intercostal diaphragmatic breathing** is the technical name for the correct method of breathing for speech. This method allows full expansion of the chest - so there is plenty of room for the lungs to expand when filled with air.

Fig 1: The Human Breathing Apparatus

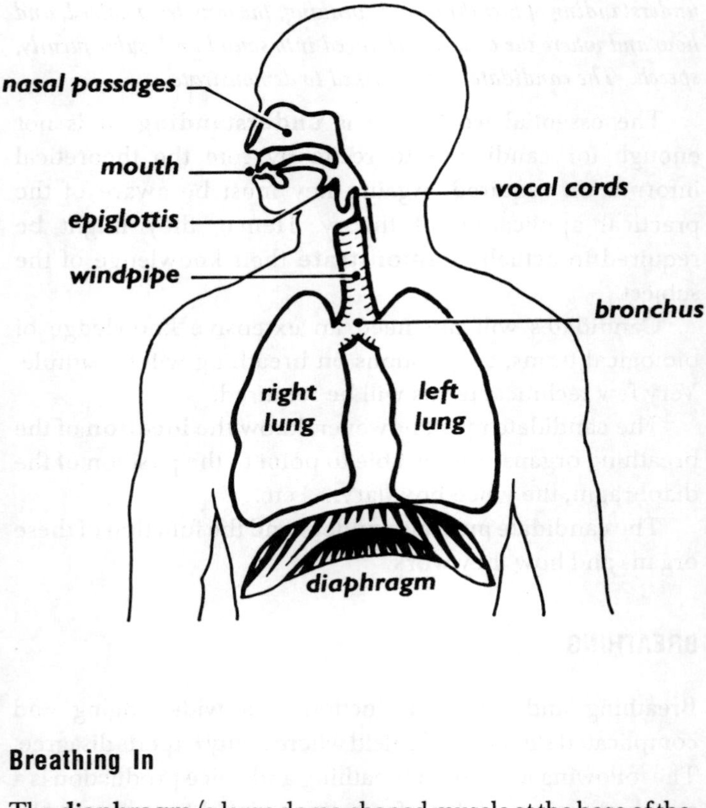

nasal passages

mouth

epiglottis

windpipe

vocal cords

bronchus

right lung

left lung

diaphragm

Breathing In

The **diaphragm** (a large dome-shaped muscle at the base of the chest) contracts and the central tendon sinks, giving downwards expansion. **The intercostal muscles** (between the ribs) lift the ribs **upwards** and **outwards** and at the same time move the edges of the diaphragm (attached to the eighth rib). This lends sideways expansion, as well as frontal expansion.

All this increases the size of the chest. The air then enters the **lungs** and fills the space. The lungs are concave and follow the shape of the inside of the chest cavity. Therefore, when the ribs move outwards and slightly upwards, the lungs follow this new shape.

Fig 2: Movement of the Diaphragm

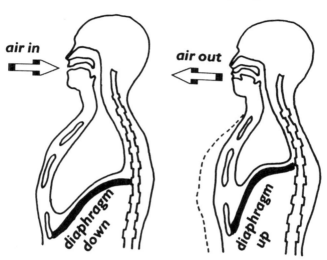

Breathing Out

The diaphragm slowly returns to its normal position. The front abdominal wall steadily contracts, controlled by the **abdominal muscles**. This process of contraction is called **abdominal press**. The ribs also return to their normal position, controlled by the abdominal muscles. All this allows air to slowly leave the lungs.

Candidates should apply this theoretical information to correct their own breathing faults.

Common Breathing Faults

Clavicular breathing - when the shoulders are raised, squeezing the diaphragm out of action and restricting full lung expansion. This results in facial strain and general tension.

Abdominal breathing - when the stomach wall is relaxed, hindering full lung expansion. The low intake of air into the lungs makes breathing shallow and uncontrolled. This causes general strain and restricts vocal range and quality.

REMEMBER - GOOD POSTURE AIDS BREATHING AND VOICE PRODUCTION.

VOICE

The air leaving the lungs passes through various passages to the **larynx**, located at the top of the **trachea** (or **windpipe**).

Fig 3: The Vocal Cords

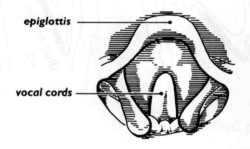

epiglottis

vocal cords

In the larynx there are two pieces of elastic tissue stretching from the front to the back. These are called the **vocal cords** or **vocal folds**. When your voice is relaxed there is a space between them - but, when speaking, they are brought together for the production of the voice. The air, passing between them, sets up vibrations. These vibrations are passed on to the column of air, which becomes voice. The vibrating columns of air are then passed through the **resonators**[5], providing **tone quality**. The main resonators are:

* the pharynx
* the mouth
* the nose
* the sinus cavities

[5] For further information consult notes for Bronze Medal

The **organs of articulation** required for correct speech are generally considered to be:

* the tongue
* the teeth
* the lips
* the hard and soft palate
* the teeth ridge (alveolar ridge)

The sound which is made into speech produces **vowel sounds** and **consonant sounds**. This information is needed to complete the whole picture, but specific questions on vowels and consonants are unlikely to be asked at this level.

Vowel Sounds

Vowels are uninterrupted sounds made by the voice. The different vowels are made by the shaping of the lips and the positioning of the tongue. There are 25 vowels in total (including the **neutral vowel, 'ER'**). These are composed of:

12 monophthongs (pure vowels)

10 diphthongs (two pure vowels joined)

3 triphthongs (three pure vowels joined, usually including the neutral vowel)

Consonant Sounds

Consonants are interrupted sounds made by the contact, or partial contact of the organs of speech (i.e. the tongue, teeth, lips, hard and soft palate).

GRADE 7

SYLLABUS

The candidate will discuss with the examiner any aspect of theory already specified for previous grades. In addition, an understanding of iambic pentameter and, where appropriate, blank verse will be expected. The Shakespeare play and the book from which the prose selection is taken must have been read in their entirety and may be discussed.

If presenting a selection from a Shakespeare play a good background knowledge of the play and the characters will be expected. Your attention is drawn to page 15 of the syllabus - Movement, Bearing and Grooming.

If the Verse and Prose selections are presented, the candidate will be expected to discuss the verse form - iambic pentameter - and sonnet form, where appropriate.

SONNET FORM

A sonnet is a poem consisting of fourteen lines of iambic pentameter. Sonnets are usually arranged into eight lines (octave) and six lines (sestet), with a pause or change of thought between the octave and sestet. There are two major sonnet forms with rhymes arranged in a definite scheme and metrical pattern:

The Petrachan or Italian Sonnet

The usual rhyme scheme in the first eight lines (octave) is *ABBA ABBA* - followed by two or three other rhymes in the final six lines (sestet): *CDE CDE* or *CD CD CD* .

The Shakespearean or Elizabethan Sonnet

This sonnet has a rhyming scheme *AB AB CD CD EF EF GG*, with the final couplet resolving the thoughts expressed in the first twelve lines.

MOVEMENT, BEARING AND GROOMING

These refer to the physical nature of the piece being performed, including:

* the **stance** - relaxed and alert

* **gesture** - when it arises naturally from the passage and the candidate's personal feeling

* any **movement** demanded by, and appropriate to the Shakespeare selection

At this grade candidates are asked to examine more thoroughly the **presentation** of their work. Not only are they now expected to understand the extract textually, but they are also expected to think about the ways in which they might bring this extract to life through use of suitable movement and gesture.

MAKE SURE THAT ALL MOVEMENT AND GESTURE IS APPROPRIATE.

All this will inevitably lead candidates to an examination of the character they are playing. Remember, all movement should be born out of the character's instinct and emotional feeling.

CHARACTER DEVELOPMENT

Here it might be useful to look at characterisation in more depth. Candidates should ask themselves key questions about the character they are playing. These questions might include:

* what motivates this character?
* why do they say the things they say?
* what is their background?
* what is their importance to the play?

BACKGROUND KNOWLEDGE OF THE PLAY

The candidate should think about:

* the context of the selection chosen - where does it fall within the general structure of the play?
* why is that particular passage important?
* what general themes does it bring out?
* what do we learn about the character in this passage?
* what happens before/after the extract?

* are there any other characters on stage? If so, to
whom is your character speaking?

STYLISTIC FEATURES

For this grade, candidates should have a working knowledge
of **blank verse (iambic pentameter)**. A line of iambic
pentameter verse is made up of five **iambic feet**. An iambic
foot is made up of one unstressed and one stressed beat. There
are five iambic feet in a line, making ten syllables per line in
total. For example:

> If <u>mu</u>sic <u>be</u> the <u>food</u> of <u>love</u>, play <u>on</u>,
> Give <u>me</u> ex<u>cess</u> of <u>it</u>; that, <u>sur</u>fei<u>ting</u>,
> The <u>appe</u>tite may <u>sick</u>en, <u>and</u> so <u>die</u>....[6]

Candidates should know how Shakespeare uses this form,
and how he varies it for dramatic effect. Candidates should
be aware of Blank Verse and the other forms Shakespeare uses
- look out for rhyming couplets, prose, songs and other
metrical verse forms. Candidates should also be able to tell
the examiner whether their extract is a soliloquy, chorus,
whether other characters are present etc.

**CANDIDATES SHOULD BE AWARE OF THE
SPECIFIC FORM USED IN THEIR SELECTIONS
AND HOW THE STYLE REFLECTS THE
THEMES AND CONTENT OF BOTH PIECES.**

GRADE 8

SYLLABUS

*The candidate will discuss with the examiner any aspect of theory
already specified for previous grades. In addition, the candidate will
be expected to show an understanding of variety in speech, which may
include pitch, pace, pause, power, inflection, tone and phrasing.
Candidates may be asked to demonstrate a simple knowledge of verse
form, with particular reference to the form of the selection chosen.*

[6]William Shakespeare, *Twelfth Night*, Act I, Scene 1

By this grade, candidates are expected to possess a broad knowledge of vocal techniques.

This theoretical knowledge should be used in conjunction with the performance of selections chosen by the candidate. If both verse and prose are performed, a detailed understanding of the verse form and prose style of the chosen selection(s) will be discussed.

Changes of pitch and pace should be observed as the speech/poem changes mood. Candidates should study the mood changes of their chosen piece. A performance is monotonous if these vocal techniques are not used. They provide interest and variety. Again, the main focus must be the **text**. All other considerations should widen out from the study of the piece itself.

In this grade, the examiner may ask questions about costume. These relate to presentation only and are **not marked**.

PHRASING

All questions will relate to phrasing in **communication**, rather than **grammar**. Punctuation is a guide to phrasing and meaning in oral work.

MODULATION

Modulation is the changing of pitch, pace, pause and power in the voice to suit the subject. It is prompted by the imagination.

PITCH

This refers to the level of the voice. The sound projected can be either high or low, according to the number of vibrations made by the vocal chords:

upper pitch: often used for excited states of mind - e.g. fear, anger, joy etc.

middle pitch: often used for ordinary conversation, narrative etc.

lower pitch: often used to express down-beat emotions, such as sorrow, sadness, despair etc.

as a general rule: the pitch of the voice should be lowered in parenthesis, and should be either raised or lowered at a change of paragraph

STRESS

There are two types of stress:

accent: stress laid on a syllable of a word. Every word of more than one syllable has one of those syllables accented, e.g. col<u>lect</u>, re<u>bel</u>

emphasis: stress laid on a word in a sentence. This helps bring out the meaning of the sentence

TONE COLOUR

This refers to the varying degrees of light and shade in the voice, prompted by the imagination.

PHRASE

This refers to the amount of text you speak in one breath. A phrase has meaning, but not always complete meaning.

PARENTHESIS

This is a word, clause, or short sentence within a long sentence. The main sentence is complete without it.

INFLECTION

This is the sliding of the voice up and down from one note to another. There are three kinds of inflection:

SIMPLE: a single slide in either direction, up or down. Used for communicating simple ideas.

simple rising: used for conveying doubt, incompleteness of expression and direct question.

simple falling: used for certainty, completeness of expression, affirmative. Also for asking questions when you have some knowledge of the answer.

DOUBLE (also known as **circumflex**): two glides in the voice, either down-up or up-down. Used when extra meaning is implied or more complex emotions are to be conveyed, e.g. sarcasm, irony, doubt.

COMPOUND: the union of more than two simple inflections. Used when conveying extreme emotions and deeper implications.

PAUSING

A pause helps bring out the sense of the words and distinguishes one phrase from another. Pauses should not all be of the same length. As a general rule, pause:

* between the subject and the verb if the subject is more than one word

* before and after simile and parenthesis

* before the final inflection in a speech or poem

* in acting - purely for dramatic effect

* before changing the pitch of the voice

The **caesura pause** is the natural pause in a line of verse. It usually follows the strongest accent, but not necessarily. It is independent of metre and can occur in the middle of a metrical foot.

The **suspensory pause** (also known as the **suspensive pause**) - when the sense of one line of the verse carries over to the next. No fresh breath is taken, but a slight pause should be maintained to keep a sense of the rhythm. This overlapping is called **enjambment**.

The **dramatic pause** - a pause for dramatic effect. Sometimes sub-divided into the following catagories:

* the **rhetorical pause** - pause placed before a word to create audience anticipation

* the **oratorical pause** - pause placed after a word to make the audience reflect on what has been said

* the **emotional pause** - to indicate an extreme emotional state. This is an illogical pause that can be placed anywhere in the sentence to indicate a character's mental confusion

MEDAL EXAMINATIONS

The discussions in the LAMDA medal examinations are much more free-form than in the grades. At this level, examiners are now more interested in the candidate's individual approach to the text. Therefore, the examiner will often ask opinionated questions designed to elicit a personal response. Candidates should research their subject matter carefully - wherever possible reading other books by the writer, examining source material etc.

BRONZE MEDAL

SYLLABUS

The candidate will discuss with the examiner any aspect of theory already specified for previous grades. In addition, the candidate will be expected to demonstrate a practical understanding of resonance and projection.

RESONANCE

Resonance is the co-vibration in the head and chest. It produces a musical and vocal tone. The resonance cavities are filled with still air. The air in these cavities vibrates and the cavities act as sound boxes for the sounds produced by the correct formation of the tongue, lips, shape of the mouth etc. The resonance cavities are:

* the **trachea/windpipe**
* pockets of the **larynx**
* the **pharynx**, divided into:

  upper pharynx, which extends from the back of the nose

  lower pharynx, which extends from the back of the mouth to the top of the larynx

* the **mouth** the most important resonator, because:

  • it is the largest

  • it is the most flexible

  • all sounds are shaped in it

  • the **hard palate** makes for brilliance of tone

  • the **soft palate** combines with the lower pharynx to produce tone colour

* the **nose**

* the **paranasal sinuses** - cavities in the bones of the skull above, on the nasal side of, and below the eye sockets, and at the back of the nose. Named after the bones in which they lie, they are:

  • the **maxillary sinuses**, found under the eye behind each cheekbone. (More specifically, they lie in the length of the lower part of the bony walls separating the nose from the eye sockets, and curve round under the eye sockets in the prominence of the cheek-bone.)

  • the **frontal sinuses**, found immediately behind the eyebrow. (More specifically, they lie behind the prominences of the eyebrows, and the forehead above the nose.)

  • the **ethmoid cells**, located behind the maxillary sinuses. (More specifically, they lie in the length of the upper part of the bony walls separating the nose from the eye sockets.)

  • the **sphenoid cells**, a large cavity behind the ethmoid cells between the back of the nose and the brain. (More specifically, they lie in the sloping wall at the back of the nose forming the roof of the upper pharynx.)

* the **thorax** - it is debatable whether this is a resonator or not. It is not a direct resonator like the hollow chambers above the larynx, but it lends sympathetic vibration to the lower notes of the voice

Fig 4: Side View of the Head

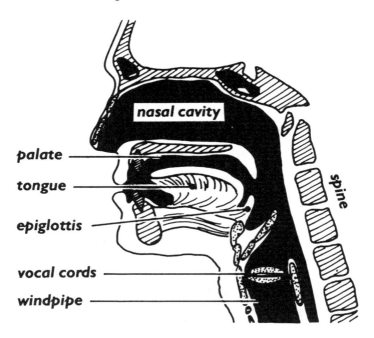

PROJECTION

Candidates should understand that projection refers not only to the production of sound, but also to the expression and communication of thoughts, feelings, meaning and style.

Vocal projection uses the muscles of breathing (using the intercostal muscles, the diaphragm and the abdominal press) to project the voice.

SILVER MEDAL

SYLLABUS

The candidate will discuss with the examiner any aspect of theory already specified for previous grades. In addition, the examiner may wish to discuss the author's style as well as their biographical details and contribution to literature.

REMEMBER THE EXAMINER MAY ASK QUESTIONS ON ANY ASPECT OF THEORY FROM PREVIOUS GRADES.

In addition, candidates should have further information on the **organs of speech**. Candidates should know how these organs are **partners in speech** e.g:

'F' is made through the contact of teeth and lips

'X' is made through contact of tongue and palate

'P' is made through contact of the lips

Fig 5: The Relationship Between the Tongue and Soft Palate When Forming Different Words

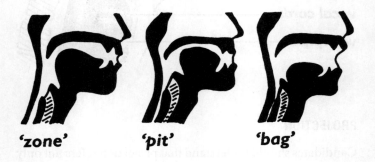

'zone'   'pit'   'bag'

At this grade, the candidate is required to research the author of their set-pieces. The syllabus provides opportunity for individual study and development. Biographical information on all authors of selections set for Silver Medal and above will be found in *Part Two* of this book.

For the Shakespeare selection, the candidate should be familiar with the life of Shakespeare, his contemporaries, and his historical context. It is also important to know the sources of the chosen play and when it was written.

For classical authors, the candidate should try and get hold of a biography of the author. If this is not possible, then the candidate should try to read other works by the author to build up a more comprehensive picture of his/her writing.

The following reference guides might prove useful for general biographical information[7]:

The Cambridge Guide to Literature in English, Ian Ousby, Cambridge University Press, 1993.

Collins Biographical Dictionary of English Literature, Antony Kamm, Harper Collins, 1993.

The Oxford Companion to English Literature, ed. Margaret Drabble, Oxford University Press, 5th edition, 1993.

For modern authors, the candidate should read the *Times Literary Supplement* and *The Times* books section for any relevant information. Also, the 'blurb' on the back of the chosen book will often give personal details about the author and list other titles.

GOLD MEDAL

SYLLABUS

The candidate will discuss with the examiner any aspect of theory already specified for previous grades. In addition, the examiner may discuss the influence of appropriate period costume for the Shakespeare selection. Candidates will be expected to understand the physical demands created by Elizabethan costume. Should they imagine the Shakespeare play to be set in some other period than the sixteenth or early seventeenth century - where the costume imposes

---

[7] There are many other reference books which candidates may find helpful - consult your local library or bookseller for specific details

different physical demands - they should be able to explain their choice, and understand its implications.

The candidate's theoretical knowledge should be fairly comprehensive at this stage. At Gold Medal level, examiners are particularly interested in the candidate's own approach to study and performance. Questions will be far-ranging and can cover all topics from previous examinations.

In preparation for this examination, candidates should try to see some productions of their chosen Shakespeare play. If this is not possible, then it is often a good idea to rent video tapes of famous past productions (the BBC now produce a Shakespeare collection on video). However, videos should never be regarded as a substitute for a careful study of the play - sometimes quite substantial cuts and changes of emphasis are made in video and film versions of the plays. For example, the popular Zeffirelli films of *Romeo and Juliet, The Taming of the Shrew* and *Hamlet* take substantial liberties with the text. The recent Ian McKellen film of *Richard III* consists of less than a quarter of the full text of the play while Olivier's famous film of the same play includes a substantial amount of material by writers other than Shakespeare.

COSTUME

Candidates might find it helpful to produce simple diagrams of their character's costume. These can be shown to the examiner so that a discussion can arise from the sketches.

If candidates are performing their selection in modern dress, they must be aware of the **original** style of presentation and costume.

SOURCES

Shakespeare draws on many diverse sources for inspiration and plot structure. These include:

* Greek tragedies
* medieval miracle and mystery plays
* medieval comedies

* influences from the European Renaissance
* the chronicles of Holinshed and Hall

The candidate should investigate the particular sources of the Shakespeare play they have chosen.

STYLE/PERIOD

Research all relevant topics, such as:

* companies of actors
* the Globe Theatre
* the Elizabethan audience
* how the plays were performed etc.

Candidates should not panic when they reach this level. They have progressed through each examination stage and should be familiar with the format by now. The Gold Medal examination is their chance to show what their personal research and emotional responses can bring to the text. Take the initiative!

SUGGESTED FURTHER READING

Teachers and students are reminded that all these books - even those which have gone out of print - will be available through public libraries. If your local main library does not hold copies, apply through the Inter-Library Loan system.

VOICE

A Guide To Practical Speech Training, Gordon Luck, (Barrie & Jenkins)

Voice and the Actor, Cicely Berry, (Harrap)

Your Voice and How To Use It Successfully, Cicely Berry, (Harrap)

The Actor and his Text, Cicely Berry (Harrap)

Clear Speech, Malcolm Morrison, (A&C Black)
The Voice Book, Michael McCallion, (Faber)

SHAKESPEARE

There are hundreds of books on Shakespeare. The following nine are considered to be particularly useful:

(i) Classic Study Texts

The Elizabethan World Picture, E. M. W. Tillyard, (Penguin)

Prefaces to Shakespeare, Harley Granville Barker, (Nick Hern Books)

Shakespeare Our Contemporary, Jan Kott, (Methuen)

Shakespearean Tragedy, A C Bradley, (MacMillan)

Shakespeare's Imagery, Caroline Spurgeon, (Cambridge University Press)

(ii) Practical Application

Playing Shakespeare, John Barton, (Methuen)

Discovering Shakespeare, A.L. Rowse, (Weidenfeld & Nicholson)

Elizabethan Stage Convention and Cue - Modern Interpreters, Alan C Desson, (Oxford University Press)

Shakespeare's English Kings, Peter Saccio, Oxford University Press)

HISTORY OF THE THEATRE

A Concise History of Theatre, Phyllis Hartnoll, (Thames and Hudson)

All The World's A Stage, Ronald Harwood, (Secker & Warburg/BBC)

A History of the Theatre, Glynne Wickham, (Cambridge University Press)

HISTORY OF ENGLISH LITERATURE

The LAMDA Guide to English Literature, (LAMDA)

A Short History of English Literature, Ifor Evans, (Penguin)

The English Novel, Walter Allen, (Penguin)

Concise Dictionary of English Literature, Oxford University Press

Pelican Guides to English Literature - several volumes covering specific periods, Boris Ford (ed), (Pelican)

THE SPEAKING OF VERSE AND PROSE

Metre Rhythm & Verse Form , New Critical Idiom series, Philip Hobsbaum, (Routledge)

Meaning, Form and Performance, Paul Ranger, (Oberon/ LAMDA)

Understanding Poetry, James Reeves, (Heinemann Educational)

The Making of Verse, Swan & Sidgwick, (Sidgwick & Jackson)

MOVEMENT

The Alexander Principle, Wilfred Barlow, (Gollancz)

The Actor and his Body, Litz Pisk, (Harrap)

A complete list of books to support all aspects of LAMDA examination work may be found on pages 72-74 of the 1996-2000 syllabus

PART TWO

BIOGRAPHICAL INFORMATION

MARTIN AMIS (born 1949)

British novelist

Born in Swansea, the son of distinguished novelist and poet, Kingsley Amis. He was educated at various schools and crammers in Britain, Spain and the USA before going to Exeter College, Oxford where he obtained a first in English Literature. He first worked as an editorial assistant on the *Times Literary Supplement* (1972-5) and was later editor for the *New Statesman*. As a journalist he has reviewed for *The Observer* and writes for the *Independent on Sunday*.

Martin Amis has had an astonishing rise to success. His first novel, *The Rachel Papers* (1973), about adolescent obsession, won the Somerset Maugham Award. Amis disassociated himself from a 1989 film version of this book. He became an 'enfant terrible' with his next book, *Dead Babies* (1975), a chilling fable as shocking as its title. *Success* (1978) was more comic. In these first books he satirises the apathy and cultural pretentiousness of metropolitan life.

Other People: A Mystery Story (1981) is a nightmarish psychological thriller. *Invasion of the Space Invaders* followed in 1982, then the richly comic *Money* (1984), set in America. In 1987 he published *Einstein's Monsters*, a collection of short stories on the theme of nuclear destruction. He has said himself that fatherhood focused his concern for the future of the world - the nuclear threat "is a background which then insidiously foregrounds itself". The nuclear theme was to emerge again in *London Fields* (1989), a surreal fable about the London underworld. This was widely admired and considered by many to be the book of the year. Controversially, it was not short-listed for the Booker Prize.

Time's Arrow (1991) was short-listed, although it did not win. In this short novel, Amis experiments with the narrative, using a reversed plot. It attracted criticism on publication for using the Holocaust as a theme for what was called 'an elegant and trivial fiction' (*Spectator*). Most of Amis's later novels have been controversial. Published in 1995, *The Information*, the story of rivalry between two bad novelists, caused a furore over the publishing rights, Amis being given a high profile by the media at the time.

As well as his novels, Amis is well known for his 'astringent' pieces of journalism. Non-fiction articles have been collected in *The Maronic Inferno* (1986), on contemporary America, and *Visiting Mrs Nabokov and other Excursions* (1993). Amis's books have been called 'enjoyably unpleasant.' His subject matter often includes destruction, decay and cruelty but he enlivens his stories with black humour ('terminally funny' *The Guardian*) and a taut, energetic prose style ('powerful and obsessive' J. G. Ballard). Amis is particularly skilful in creating grotesque characters (eg. Keith Talent in *London Fields*) and is able (like his father) to capture and exaggerate the manner in which people speak. He uses language extravagantly. 'Amis's figures, like those of Dickens, are caricatures that have their own gigantic reality' - Julian Symons in *The London Review*. As a novelist, Amis is versatile, controversial and considered to be at the forefront of his generation of writers. His critics feel that his preoccupation with 'designer violence' and a tendency to sententiousness undermine his talent.

MATTHEW ARNOLD (1822-1888)

British poet and critic

Born at Laleham, Middlesex, son of Thomas Arnold, the education reformer and great headmaster of Rugby. Matthew was educated at Winchester, Rugby and Balliol College, Oxford. He became a fellow of O'Neil College in

1845 and was later appointed Private Secretary to Lord Lansdowne. Arnold was considered something of a dandy and enjoyed being sought after by London society. He died of heart failure whilst running for a tram in 1888.

He travelled in the late 1840s, meeting a Swiss girl, Marguerite, who inspired much of his early lyric poetry. In 1851, when he decided to marry Frances Lucy Wightman, Lord Lansdowne obtained for him an Inspectorship of schools. He held this post for thirty-five years, until his retirement. During these years he travelled throughout the country, observing extreme social conditions which would prove a source of material for his writings. He made extensive studies in an effort to improve education, particularly secondary education. He believed in better organisation and that England should look to European models. His recommendations have become standard texts.

Arnold's first two collections of verse, *The Strayed Reveller and Other Poems* (1849) and *Empedocles on Etna and Other Poems* (1852), were published anonymously, meeting with little success. After his appointment to Inspector of schools, he re-published these volumes under his own name and began to achieve recognition. *Poems, A New Edition* (which he prefaced with his own ideas on poetic practice) appeared in 1853. There followed *Poems Second Series* (1855) and his last volume, *New Poems* (1867).

Arnold's poetical works are not extensive but there is much variety of expression within them - lyricism in the *Marguerite* poems, *The Forsaken Merman, Dover Beach* and *Philomela;* poetic drama in *Empedocles on Etna* and *Merope;* narrative poems like *Tristram and Iseult* and *Sohrab and Rustum;* elegies, such as *Thyrsis, The Scholar Gypsy* and *Memorial Verses.* In subject matter and melodic style, Arnold showed a fondness for the classics, particularly for Greek poetry, which he often used as a model. Meditative and often melancholy, his poems have been described as having a 'despairing gentleness'. The finest of them are often personal and reflect inner conflicts or the conflict between science and art. In *The Scholar Gypsy* he looks back from the turmoil of modern times to a period of simple faith. *Dover Beach,* perhaps his greatest poem, was written on his honeymoon while staying at a seaside hotel. It epitomises the uncertainty of religion in a society rapidly being changed by the new industrial age. He longed for a self-confident religious faith and greatly admired the 'calmness' of his friend, the poet Wordsworth. The *Memorial Verses,* written in 1850, were a lament for his death.

In recognition of Arnold's contribution to literature, he was appointed Professor of Poetry at Oxford in 1857, a position he held for ten years (while still continuing his duties as Inspector of schools).

For much of his later life, apart from the 1867 volume, Arnold concentrated on writing prose. He became an influential voice in literary criticism and expressed forthright opinions on the religious, social, political and educational issues of his day. *Essays in Criticism* (1865 and posthumously in 1888) contains the best of his critical work. In these essays, he argued that England needed more intellectual curiosity and advocated a broader European outlook, attacking 'provincialism' and 'Philistinism' - a lack of real knowledge. He wrote freely on theological and political themes in *Culture and Anarchy* (1869) and *Literature and Dogma* (1873). In the first of these, the prose work which established him as a social critic, he expands on his concern for spiritual anarchy expressed at the end of *Dover Beach.* He recommends culture as 'the great help out of our present difficulties.' Arnold defines culture as 'the pursuit of total perfection by means of getting to know, on all the matters which most concern us, the best which has been thought and said in the world'.

As a literary critic and as a Victorian, Arnold was a man in conflict, neither sharing the materialism of the nineteenth century nor the subjectivity of Romanticism. He points out in *The Study of Poetry* (1880) that art should not stand by merit alone but should be discussed in terms of its moral function. He talks of the problems of writing poetry in an 'age wanting in moral grandeur'. In later life the differences between rational opinion and religious faith tormented him. Despite the occasional remoteness of their subject matter, Arnold's prose writings have a clear lucid style, often enlivened by his elegant, ironic humour. His opinions are always expressed in a forthright and articulate manner. Many twentieth century writers, among them F. R. Leavis and T. S. Eliot, have been influenced by them.

W. H. (Wystan Hugh) AUDEN (1907-73)
British-born poet, dramatist and critic, later an American citizen

Born in York, the son of a doctor, Auden was educated at Gresham's School, Holt and Christ Church, Oxford. After university, he lived for some time in Berlin, returning to England in 1929 to take up teaching.

His first volume was *Poems* (1930), initially published privately by his friend Stephen Spender while at Oxford, followed by *The Orators* (1932). *Look Stranger!* (1936) established him as a most influential and able poet. The poems were full of original lyrics, technical mastery and 'a voice which impressed readers of the 1930s as a civilised reply to the stridency of fascism'. He became a leading voice of the younger generation and the key member of a group that formed a new movement in poetry. Influenced by the poetry of T. S. Eliot and Gerard Manley Hopkins, and the politics of Karl Marx, the 'Auden generation' (or 'Pylon School' as it was termed by its critics for its use of industrial imagery) consisted of Stephen Spender, Cecil Day Lewis and Louis MacNeice. In 1932, Auden started writing experimental plays for the Group Theatre in London. These include *The Dance of Death* (1933) and, in collaboration with Christopher Isherwood, *The Dog Beneath the Skin* (1935), *The Ascent of F6* (1936) and *On the Frontier* (1938).

Auden travelled to Spain in support of the Republican cause during the Spanish Civil War. This gave rise to *Spain*

(1937). Other travels gave rise to *Letters from Ireland* (1937 - written with Louis MacNeice) and *Journey to War* (1939 - an account of his visit to China with Christopher Isherwood). In 1937 he was awarded the King's Medal for poetry and the following year he edited the *Oxford Book of Light Verse.*

A major turning point in his life came when he left England for the USA with Christopher Isherwood at the start of 1939. He became a U.S. citizen in 1946. After teaching for a time in America, he became a freelance writer. This period saw a marked change in his work. With a return to his Anglican faith, Auden's work became more reflective, dismissing the Marxism of the earlier poems. He extensively edited many early poems when *Collected Poems of W. H. Auden* was published in 1945. Poetry collections from the American period include *Another Time* (1940), *The Double Man* (1941 - the title signifying his own personal search for belief and logic) and *The Age of Anxiety* (1948), which won the Pulitzer Prize for poetry. His tone grew more wry and ironic as he aged, the poems themselves more domestic and intimate.

Later volumes include *The Shield of Achilles* (1955), *The Old Man's Rod* (1956), *Homage to Clio* (1960), *About the House* (1965), *City Without Walls* (1969), *Academic Graffiti* (1972), and *Epistle to a Godson* (1972).

Auden's post-war critical work is collected in such volumes as *The Enchanted Flood* (1950), *The Dyer's Hand* (1962) and *Secondary World* (1968). He also wrote a series of dramatic monologues based on Shakespeare's *The Tempest* called *For the Time Being, A Christmas Oratorio* and *The Sea and the Mirror* (1944). His musical interests resulted in a collaboration with Chester Kallman on the libretto for Stravinsky's opera *The Rake's Progress* (1951). Benjamin Britten, who had written incidental music for some of the early plays, based his first opera, *Paul Bunyan* (1941), on a script by Auden.

Auden divided his final years between homes in Greenwich Village, New York City and Kirchstetten, Austria. During his lifetime he received various literary awards. He was elected Professor of Poetry at Oxford in 1956 and became a Fellow of Christ Church in 1962. He returned to his college in Oxford in 1972 and remained there until his death. *Collected Poems* (1976) was published posthumously.

Auden's poetry falls into two main periods: the period during the 30s, fired by left wing idealism (which is full of bold images and phrases and an intellectual approach that marked him as T. S. Eliot's successor) and the period in America during the 40s which reflects the change of attitude of an older man in a stable society: more conservative, more reflective. The later poems may not be as stimulating as the earlier ones but they are well-crafted and show the same inquisitive mind. Spender described Auden as the most accomplished technician of his day. Throughout his career he was an experimenter in verse form, with a fine ear for the rhythm and music of words. His style ranges from the light lyric to cynical satire, with the vigour of everyday idiom and vocabulary. Auden's poetic output was considerable, with themes both personal and public and a voice both 'colloquial and magisterial'. It was the hope of his generation to make poetry more acceptable to the common man. It is not with the earlier, more public, poetry that he achieved this - their appeal was to the more sophisticated, intellectual reader. He achieved his greatest popularity with the rather more private, tender lyrics which are not concerned with sociological theories.

JANE AUSTEN (1775 - 1817)

British novelist

Born at Steventon, Hampshire, the sixth of seven children born to the Reverend George Austen, a country clergyman. She spent the first twenty-five years of her life at the rectory in Steventon and, encouraged by her father, read widely, especially the novels of Richardson, Fielding, Sterne and Fanny Burney and the poetry of Cowper, Crabbe and Scott.

Austen began writing at an early age. These juvenilia were often parodies of the excesses of contemporary fiction, such as gothic romances. Among these, *Love and Friendship* was written when she was 14, *A History of England (by a partial, ignorant and prejudiced historian)* at 15, *A Collection of Letters* at 16 and *Lady Susan* at 17. When she was 21 she embarked on the first drafts of *Pride and Prejudice, Sense and Sensibility* and *Northanger Abbey* only to have the first of these turned down by the publisher. *Northanger Abbey* was purchased for £10 but not then printed. She abandoned writing for a time.

In 1801 the family moved to Bath and, after her father's death, to Southampton. In 1809 they moved to Chawton Cottage near Alton, which was owned by her brother. During these years, Austen's only creative effort was an unfinished story, *The Watsons*. It was not until she was 36 that any of her novels were published. *Sense and Sensibility* appeared in 1811, *Pride and Prejudice* followed in 1813, *Mansfield Park* in 1814, *Emma* in 1816, *Persuasion* and *Northanger Abbey* a year after her death. The novels were not written in this order. *Sense and Sensibility* is a reworked version of *Eleanor and Marianne*, written 1795-6, and *Pride and Prejudice* was revised from *First Impressions* written in 1797.

Austen's health began to fail as she was writing *Emma*. She died at Winchester in 1817 at the age of 41, leaving an unfinished novel, *Sanditon*. In her later years, apart from trips to London and to Bath, she spent most of her time at Chawton (*Mansfield Park, Emma* and *Persuasion* were all written in the family parlour there), content to live within the confines of her family to whom - particularly her sister Cassandra - she was devoted.

She never married, although there is evidence of one brief attachment. There is a belief that her own love is reflected in that of Anne Elliot in *Persuasion*. Austen had many admirers, including Sir Walter Scott who praised her for 'that exquisite touch which renders ordinary common-place things and characters interesting'. The Prince Regent kept a set of her novels at each of his residences. She had a few critics too. Charlotte Bronte, Elizabeth Barrett Browning and D.H. Lawrence found her limitations too great, restricting her concerns to such a small section of society. However, for the majority of her readers it is such detailed focus that makes her unique. She regarded herself as a miniaturist working, as she put it herself, a 'little bit (two inches wide) of ivory'. She wrote about what was familiar to her - the provincial middle-class life of Regency England; of family and human affairs (public events are seldom mentioned) - and of this her knowledge is deep and true. 'Three or four families in a country village is the very thing to work on,' she wrote in 1814. She was a strong social observer. Her characters are developed with minuteness and accuracy so that they are not types but individuals. Her witty observations (particularly of female characters) and delicate irony enrich the novels with subtle humour. The light wit became sharper in the later novels, where follies and vanities are more keenly scrutinised. Her plots are carefully constructed and she had a gift for dialogue.

In 1870, her nephew, J. Austen-Leigh, published a *Memoir*, which started a Jane Austen following. Her reputation has increased in the twentieth century and she is now considered one of the greatest figures in English literature. She brought the English novel to maturity and paved the way for its development throughout the nineteenth century. It is ironic that her novels, once considered of 'limited' interest by her critics are, following recent television and film adaptations, currently enjoying such overwhelming and widespread popularity.

JUDITH BEHRENDT (born 1947)

Belize-born poet

Judith Behrendt began her literary career at the age of 16 and has been greatly influenced by the work of Anais Nin. She has published short stories and poems in *The Feminist Voice.*

The poem, *Nasarayaba,* is contained in the anthology, *Creation Fire: A CAFRA Anthology of Caribbean Women's Poetry,* edited by Ramabai Espinet. CAFRA - The Caribbean Association for Feminist Research and Action, was founded in 1985. It is a membership association of individual feminists, women activists and women's organisations which spans the Dutch, English, French and Spanish speaking Caribbean and its diaspora.

Judith Behrendt says that she was 'born a feminist, poet, writer, dreamer'. She works in family planning, 'to help women control their fertility,' which she believes is essential to equality.

ARNOLD BENNETT (1867 - 1931)

British novelist, short-story writer, playwright and journalist

Born in Hanley, Staffordshire into a strict Wesleyan Methodist home. He was educated in Newcastle-under-Lyme where he studied law and started work in his father's solicitors office. When he was 21 he set off for London, hoping to become a writer but progress was slow. He eventually managed to break into journalism by becoming Assistant Editor and later Editor of *Woman* magazine (1896-1900).

A short story, *A Letter Home*, was accepted by *The Yellow Book* and a first autobiographical novel, *The Man from the North*, was published in 1898. Bennett began to experiment with narrative prose and both *The Grand Babylon Hotel* and *Anna of the Five Towns*, which vary greatly in content and style, were published in 1902.

In the same year, Bennett moved to France and settled in Paris. He later married a Frenchwoman, Marguerite Soulie. Bennett had long been an admirer of French culture, particularly the French realistic novels of Zola, Maupassant and Flaubert where the environment has a strong influence on the characters. It was in this style, while living in France, that he wrote his next novels, which were to prove his best. The 'five towns' of the Potteries (now Stoke-on-Trent), referred to in *Anna of the Five Towns,* are the grim, industrial area where Bennett had grown up. These were also to provide the background for *The Old Wives' Tale* (1908). His greatest achievements, and the books which turned him from a successful to a famous novelist, are *Clayhanger* (1910), its sequel *Hilda Lessways* (1911) and *These Twain* (1916). These were subsequently republished as *The Clayhanger Family* (1925). Two collections of short stories *Tales of the Five Towns* (1905) and *The Grim Smile of the Five Towns* (1907) are set in the same region, as are several minor poems. 'He is to the Black Country what Hardy is to Wessex'.

Although Bennett returned to England and settled in Kent in 1912, he never returned to live in the Midlands. During the 1914-18 War, he served as Director of Propaganda in the Ministry of Information but declined a knighthood at the end of 1918.

Bennett was prolific and versatile as a writer, the author of some eighty novels, short stories, essays, articles and plays. Many of these were 'pot-boilers', but they gave him the celebrity and luxurious lifestyle he craved. He had a passionate interest in the theatre, gave patronage to many theatrical enterprises and was actively involved with the management of the Lyric Theatre, Hammersmith. *Milestones* (1912), which he co-wrote, was his most popular play and *Riceyman Steps* (1923) the best of the later novels. *Lord Raingo* (1926), a political novel satirising society, was influenced by his friendship with Lord Beaverbrook who had encouraged the 'Books and Persons' series that he wrote for *The Evening Standard* from 1926 until his death from typhoid.

Bennett is reminiscent of Dickens in his eye for detail, the understanding of the society in which he grew up and the lives of the ordinary characters who populate his greatest novels. He describes the dilemmas and aspirations of their lives with warmth and humour. He noted in his diary that the essential characteristic of the really great novelist is, 'a Christ-like all embracing compassion'. For realism he stands alongside John Galsworthy and H.G. Wells.

Other novels include *The Card* (1911), *The Roll Call* (1918), *The Pretty Lady* (1918) and *Mr. Prohack* (1922). Other plays are *The Honeymoon* (1912), *The Great Adventure* (1913 - based on one of his own novels) and *The Love Match* (1922). He was disappointed about his lack of success as a dramatist. Short stories and articles include *The Truth About an Author* (1903) and *The Author's Craft* (1914). His journal began in 1896 and was published in 1932-3. It is written 'in the manner of a modern Pepys,' according to his editor, Newman Flower, and reveals much about the man himself - his love of France, what he ate and the plays and novels he enjoyed. Interestingly, he meticulously records the number of words written when working on a novel: in 1908 it was 423,500.

A popular leading literary figure of his day, Bennett influenced the development of the English regional novel.

JAMES BOSWELL (1740 - 95)
Scottish journal writer and biographer of Samuel Johnson

Born in Edinburgh to a family descended from Scottish gentry. His father, a judge, was Lord Auchinleck. Educated at Edinburgh High School and the Universities of Edinburgh and Glasgow, where he studied law.

Shunning the legal career his father planned for him, Boswell started mixing in social circles that might influence his literary and political ambitions. In 1760, Boswell moved to London, after the commencement of what was a long battle of wills with his father - who thought him feckless and extravagant. He briefly converted to the Catholic faith. He spent much time in Newmarket cultivating the society of 'the great, the gay and ingenious'.

It was in a London bookshop that he met the great Dr. Johnson. Boswell was only 22 and, unperturbed by preliminary snubs, Dr Johnson and he became friends. Dr. Johnson is reported to have said, "Give me your hand, I have taken a liking to you". It was an unlikely friendship between a great moralist, devout Christian and English Tory (Johnson) and a dissolute, radical, Scottish Whig (Boswell) but the pair became constant companions. Boswell recorded conversations and anecdotes that would illustrate Johnson's 'majestic character.' He planned to write his biography soon after their first meeting.

Encouraged by Johnson, Boswell recorded his elaborate view of contemporary London life, published in 1950 as *Boswell's London Journal 1762-3*. Between 1763 and 1766 he toured the continent, studying law in Utrecht. He met Rousseau, Voltaire and, in Corsica, General Paoli - whose cause he supported in *An Account of Corsica* (1768). Boswell's eye for detail and vivacious prose style established him as a man of letters.

His mother's death brought him back to Edinburgh in 1766 where, to his father's relief, he began to practise as an advocate. In 1767 he published *Dorando*, an allegorical romance. In 1769 he married his cousin and appeared to settle down. However, he kept another home in London to which he escaped whenever he could. This enabled him to move in literary circles, pursue sensual and intellectual pleasures and enjoy the company of Johnson, a father figure who was more congenial than his own. In 1773 he was elected to 'The Club' which Sir Joshua Reynolds, the painter, had founded. Here he enjoyed the company of Goldsmith, Garrick and Burke; Dr. Johnson called him 'Bozzy that clubable man'.

In the same year Johnson and Boswell travelled to the Scottish Hebrides, the tour resulting in two books: Dr. Johnson's *Journal to the Western Isles* (1775) and Boswell's *Journal of the Tour of the Hebrides* (1785). Between 1777 and 1783 Boswell wrote essays in *The London Magazine* under the name 'Hypochondriac' while continuing his legal career in Scotland. He succeeded to his father's estate in 1782.

Johnson died in 1784, an emotional blow from which Boswell never recovered. He was called to the English Bar in 1786 but his aspirations for a political career failed. Despite his depression and bouts of drinking, he started to organise the wealth of material he had gathered and began to compile *The Life of Samuel Johnson LLD*, with encouragement from the scholar Edmond Malone. After much delay, this was published in 1791 and remains one of the greatest biographies ever written. It is a unique record of the literary and social scene of eighteenth century England which has as much vivid appeal to the twentieth century as it had then. Boswell boasted, when he had finished, that he had "Johnsonised the land - and I trust they will not only talk, but think, Johnson".

Boswell died worn out, a broken man, in 1795. He had superb gifts as a reporter and held back no secrets regarding his own life. As a result, he has given us a unique self-portrait in his letters to two university friends, in the private papers and in the journals which he kept after 1762. These were not published until the twentieth century. Boswell describes, with great honesty, his bouts of manic depression, dissipation and promiscuity. He also reveals himself as a talented writer worthy of being remembered in his own right and not merely as Dr. Johnson's biographer.

> "I am absolutely certain that my mode of biography, which gives not only a history of Johnson's visible progress through the world, and of his publications, but a view of his mind in his letters and conversations, is the most perfect that can be conceived and will be more of a life than any work that has ever yet appeared."
>
> James Boswell

> "He was an extraordinary bundle of paradoxes, and perhaps it is this that makes him so perennially interesting. Loving husband and father, dissipated whore-chaser, conscientious lawyer, drunken buffoon, writer of tedious doggerel and of one of the finest biographies in the English language."
>
> David Daiches on James Boswell

ANITA BROOKNER (born 1928)

British novelist

Born in London, daughter of Polish-Jewish parents. Educated at James Allen's Girls School, King's College, University of London and the Courtauld Institute of Art.

She first gained recognition as an art historian, lecturing at the University of Reading and the Courtauld Institute of Art before becoming the first woman Slade Professor of Art at Cambridge (1967-68). Her books on art history have established her international reputation as an authority on late eighteenth century and early nineteenth century French painting.

Since she turned to writing fiction in 1980, she has enjoyed a rapid rise to success, producing a novel each year: *A Start in Life* (1981), *Providence* (1982), *Look at Me* (1983), *Hotel du Lac* (1984 - winner of the Booker Prize and filmed for television in 1986), *Family and Friends* (1985), *Misalliance* (1986), *A Friend from England* (1987), *Latecomers* (1988), *Lewis Percy* (1989), *Brief Lives* (1990), *A Closed Eye* (1991), *Fraud* (1992) and *Family Romance* (1993), *A Private View* (1994), *Incidents in the Rue Laugier* (1995) and *Altered States* (1996).

Themes of betrayal, disillusionment and disappointment in love are common to many of the novels. Her heroines, too, have many similarities. They are usually intelligent, solitary but sensitive women longing for love and companionship but with neither great beauty nor the boldness to get what they want out of life. Brookner has said in interviews that five of the novels do, indeed, contain sections of what appears to be autobiography: the woman is middle-aged, professional (even a novelist sometimes), financially independent and from an academic upper middle-class background. In *Family and Friends* (1985), Brookner turned the focus away from one woman and onto a family, basing the saga on her own East European ancestry.

The underlying theme of all her books is that those who are good, yet vulnerable, do not win the prizes in life. Rather, they are exploited by the less scrupulous and more ruthless. The painful discovery of this truth forms the basis for many of her novels and is told with a balance of comedy and pessimism. Most of the novels are short, written in an elegant style that has been admired for its wit and perception of human behaviour. Her writing is full of literary allusions (reflecting her scholarly background) and precise visual details (reflecting her art critic's eye).

Some of Brookner's critics have found that the sharp humour of the early books is not evident in the later novels. Her early novels have been compared to those of Barbara Pym. This does not please her. Rosamond Lehmann, Elizabeth Taylor and Edith Templeton are the English novelists she most admires.

Anita Brookner still lectures and writes on art history and is a regular reviewer of fiction for *The Spectator*. She was awarded the CBE in 1990.

JOHN CASSIDY (born 1928)

British poet

John Cassidy lives in Lancashire, where he is a lecturer in literature and drama at a tertiary college. His poems have appeared in many magazines and anthologies and have been broadcast on radio and television. A selection of his work was included in *Poetry Introduction 3* (Faber, 1975). Cassidy's booklet, *The Dancing Man,* was the first Poet's Yearbook Award publication in 1977.

His first full length collection, *An Attitude of Mind,* was published by Hutchinson in 1978. Two pamphlets, *Changes of Light* and *The Fountain,* were published by Bloodaxe Books in 1979. Cassidy's second book-length collection, *Night Cries*, also published by Bloodaxe in 1982, was a Poetry Book

Society recommendation. His third book of poems, *Walking on Frogs*, was favourably received by the critics.

'A strong, delicate volume of nature poetry ... a kind of *Lyrical Ballads* of our time'

Terry Eagleton

'Precise observation and compassion'

Iain Crichton Smith

'John Cassidy has never had the recognition he deserves. His work has often been overshadowed by that of flashier and more fashionable writers, and he's not a member of the poetry circus which hogs the limelight at festivals etc. In a world where bright sparks from arts associations offer ideas like 'poetry and bingo' (no I haven't made it up, either), Cassidy has quietly followed his own path and has concentrated on honesty, integrity and the craft of writing ....'

Jim Burns

JUNG CHANG (born 1952)

Chinese novelist

Jung Chang was born at Yibin in the Sichuan Province of China. Before she became a student, she had a series of menial jobs and for a brief period during her teens was a Red Guard. She went to Sichuan University to study English and, awarded a scholarship by York University, left China for Britain in 1978. It was at York that she gained a PhD in Linguistics in 1982, the first person from the People's Republic of China to do so from a British University. She has now made London her home and teaches at the School of Oriental and African Studies, part of London University.

In 1992 Jung Chang won the NCR Book Award and, in the following year, the British Book of the Year Award for her autobiographical *Wild Swans*. This is a personal account of her own and her family's life in twentieth century China. In recording the pains (and occasional pleasures) on the road to survival, she proves an admirable storyteller - full of honesty, humour and intelligence. The book became a best-seller, critically acclaimed for its style, much admired for its spirit.

'Immensely moving and unsettling; an unforgettable portrait of the brain-death of a nation'

J. G. Ballard in *The Sunday Times*.

'*Wild Swans* made me feel like a five year old. This is a family memoir that has the breadth of the most enduring social histories.'

Martin Amis in the *Independent on Sunday*

SAMUEL TAYLOR COLERIDGE (1772 - 1834)

British poet, critic and philosopher

Born in Ottery St. Mary, Devon, the thirteenth son of a country clergyman, he was educated at Christ's Hospital, London. Here he met Charles Lamb and was known as a brilliant conversationalist but also 'a playless day-dreamer'. He went to Jesus College, Cambridge and showed great promise. He got into debt, however, and, swept up with revolutionary ideals, left to join the army. He did not return to take his degree.

In 1794 he met the poet Robert Southey in Oxford and struck up a friendship. Together they formed plans for setting up a Utopian community in America. This dream failed. Southey persuaded Coleridge to marry his fiancée's sister - it proved an unhappy relationship. Coleridge became a freelance journalist and lecturer. In 1796 he published *Poems on Various Subjects* (1796). It was at this time, due to ill health and depression, that he also started taking opium (laudanum).

In 1796 the Coleridges moved to Nether Stowey on the edge of the Quantock Hills in Somerset. It was here that his friendship with William Wordsworth and his sister, Dorothy, began. This was to mark the beginning of a literary partnership, during which Coleridge produced his best work.

In 1798, Wordsworth and Coleridge together produced *Lyrical Ballads*, one of the most influential volumes of poetry ever written. It broke away from tradition and signalled the beginning of Romanticism. The poets' contributions were sharply contrasting. Wordsworth's poetry dealt with nature and the ordinary. It was agreed that Coleridge's endeavours should be directed to persons and characters supernatural or at least romantic. Although Coleridge contributed only four to Wordsworth's nineteen poems, he was responsible for one of the most memorable in the collection, *The Rime of the Ancient Mariner*. This, his most famous poem, is a parable about a nightmarish sea voyage. His other poems in the collection are *The Nightingale, The Foster-Mother's Tale* and *The Dungeon*.

During this creative period he began other ballads in a similar idiom to *The Ancient Mariner*, though they were not completed. In 1797 he wrote the first part of *Christabel,* a romantic narrative that has elements of magic. He completed the second part in 1800, yet it remained unpublished until 1816. *Kubla Khan,* an exotic, enigmatic piece written in 1798, was never finished. Coleridge claimed that he had woken from a dream with a poem in his head, but 'a person from Porlock,' a nearby village, had interrupted him while he was writing it down. After the interruption, he could never recapture the dream. During this period, Coleridge also wrote a sequence of 'conversation' poems, addressed to friends. *Fears in Solitude, This Lime Tree Bower, My Prison* and *Frost at Midnight,* addressed to his son Hartley, are among them.

In 1800 both the Coleridges and the Wordsworths moved to the Lake District. By early 1801 Coleridge already believed that 'the poet is dead in me ... I was once a volume of gold leaf rising and riding on every breath of fancy'. He became infatuated with Wordsworth's sister-in-law, Sara Hutchinson, but his passion was unrequited. He addressed to her his 1802 poem, *Dejection: An Ode*. This sad, emotional piece is probably his last great poem. By now his opium-taking had become an addiction, often giving him nightmares.

Weakened by illness, he went to Malta in 1804, remaining there until 1807. On his return, he separated from his wife and wandered the country, staying with various friends. He stayed with the Wordsworths at Dove Cottage for two years. During this period (1808-10) he brought out *The Friend*, a literary, moral and political periodical which he dictated to Sara Hutchinson. When Sara left the Lake District, Coleridge moved to London in some distress. He was hurt by Wordsworth's complaint that he was a domestic 'nuisance.' A rift grew between the two men.

In London, Coleridge continued lecturing, writing a few poems and government articles. In 1813 his play, *Remorse* (a re-working of an earlier piece, *Osirio*), was staged at Drury Lane. After a mental breakdown later that year, he spent the summer of 1814 with friends in Bath. Here he wrote three short critical essays, wrote marginal notes to *The Rime of the Ancient Mariner* and his volume of criticism, *Biographia Literaria* (published in 1817). This is an extraordinary critical work in which Coleridge presents his own literary biography, as well as his views. The last chapters are devoted to his theory of Romanticism. It established his reputation as a man of great knowledge and insight. In 1816, with encouragement from Byron, *Christabel and Other Poems* was finally published. This volume included *Kubla Khan* and *The Pains of Sleep*. The first edition of his collected poems, *Sibylline Leaves*, also appeared.

Late in 1816, he went to live with the surgeon James Gillman in Highgate. Though Coleridge was a patient, Gillman treated him as a member of his own family. He received many visitors, being something of a literary legend to his younger disciples. Carlyle christened him 'The Sage of Highgate' and Lamb, dedicating his *Essays of Elia* to him, called him 'an archangel a little damaged'. Coleridge's later prose concentrated on religious and social matters and he died at Highgate, his brilliance as a conversationalist set down in *Table Talk* (1836), published after his death.

Wordsworth called him 'the most wonderful man I have ever known'. He was certainly a very educated and eloquent man with wide-ranging talents. A poet, journalist and critic, he was also a philosopher who wrote numerous social, religious and political essays. In his later years he became a distinguished lecturer, particularly on the works of Shakespeare for which he drew large audiences. These lectures were published as *Shakespearean Criticism* in 1907. The sheer breadth of his work and of his vision perhaps diffused his creative talent, although some have put the fragmentary nature of his work down to a lack of moral resolution. His reputation as a poet is based on a brief blossoming, a small output which served to make him, together with William Wordsworth, the great progenitor of English Romanticism.

e. e. (edward estlin) cummings (1894-1962)

American poet, novelist and artist

Born in Cambridge, Massachusetts, the son of a teacher who later became a minister. He attended Harvard and while there, together with fellow student John Dos Passos, published *Eight Harvard Poets* (1917). In this volume he makes use of the lower case, 'the beginning of my style'. He drove with the volunteer ambulance corps in France during World War I. He was wrongfully accused of treason and kept in a French detention centre. This experience was recounted in his first book, an autobiographical novel, *The Enormous Room* (1922). In this, he first established the theme that was to influence his later work - a commitment to the free, the individual and idiosyncratic and an aversion to bureaucracy, prudishness and over-intellectualising.

He remained in Paris after the war, meeting Ezra Pound and making a living painting and writing humorous articles for *Vanity Fair*. His first book of poetry was *Tulips and Chimneys* (1923), strongly influenced by the English Romantic poets. This was followed by several collections of mainly short lyric verse: *XLI Poems*, *&* and *is 5* (all 1925). These show greater experimentation with the punctuation, grammar and typographical techniques with which cummings is identified - establishing his individualism by using lower case letters in his name. He surprised and sometimes scandalised with his frank vocabulary and caustic satire.

Other poetical works include *Viva* (1931), *no thanks* (1935 - dedicated to those who refused to publish him), *1/20* (1936), *Collected Poems* (1938), *50 Poems* (1940), *IXI* (1944), *Poems 1923-54* (1954) and *Ninety-Five Poems* (1958). Posthumous publications include *73 poems* (1963), *Complete Poems 1913-63* (1972). *Complete Poems 1904-62* (1994) collected everything in one volume. His selected letters were published in 1969. Non-poetical works include *Him* (1927), a drama in verse and prose, a book with no title (1936) and *Eimi* (Greek for 'I am'), published in 1933, a travel diary based on a trip to the Soviet Union in 1931. His bitter impressions of the regimentation and suppression he witnessed there caused a break from socialism and his subsequent work is more reactionary. *Tom,* a satirical ballad based on *Uncle Tom's Cabin* was published in 1935 and a collection of his art appears in *CIOPW* (1931). The title of the latter refers to the various media he utilises for his drawings - in charcoal, ink, oil, pencil and water-colour.

His reputation grew in the 1950s and from 1952-3 he was the Charles Eliot Norton Professor of Poetry at Harvard. *I: six non lectures* (1953) are based on his work there. cummings's experimental style, very much influenced by contemporary jazz, free verse and slang, is distinguished by unusual punctuation; the division of words and phrases by parentheses; typographical oddities; the frequent use of puns and a blend of stanza and free verse; and the design on the page is often a visual manifestation of the theme or tone of the poem. The oddities are used to support what are largely conventional lyrics (love poems, short satirical pieces) and sometimes distract from their depth and simplicity. cummings opened up new possibilities and has influenced other poets in America and Britain.

C. (Cecil) DAY LEWIS (1904-72)

British poet, novelist and critic

Born in County Sligo, Ireland, the son of a Church of Ireland minister. He was educated at Sherborne School before going to Wadham College, Oxford. Here he met W.H. Auden (q.v.) and Stephen Spender. Lewis became associated with a group of left wing poets, of which Auden was the leader, who made a great impact in the 1930s. Their major influences were Eliot and Karl Marx. In 1936 Day Lewis joined the Communist party.

From 1927 to 1935 he was engaged with teaching and writing. *Transitional Poem* (1929) was followed by *From Feathers to Iron* (1931), *The Magnetic Mountain* (1933), *A Time to Dance* (1935) and *Noah and the Waters* (1936). During the 30s, Day Lewis wrote detective fiction under the pseudonym of 'Nicholas Blake'. *A Question of Proof* (1935) was his first work in the genre. *The Friendly Tree* (1936) was the first of three largely autobiographical novels. *Overture to Death* (1938) and *Poems in Wartime* reflect the uncertainties of the times.

During World War II, Day Lewis edited material for the Ministry of Information (1941-46). In 1946 he was invited to give the Clark Lectures at Cambridge; he was subsequently Professor of Poetry at Oxford (1951-56), Charles Eliot Norton Professor of Poetry at Harvard (1964-65), and Vice-President of the Royal Society of Literature from 1958. On the death of John Masefield in 1968, he was appointed Poet Laureate. Day Lewis's second marriage in 1951, to the actress Jill

Balcon, increased his interest in the spoken word and he frequently gave poetry recitals.

Collections of original verse include *An Italian Visit* (1953) and the last volume of poetry, *The Whispering Roots* (1970).

CHARLES DICKENS (1812-70)

British novelist

Born in Portsea, Hampshire, the son of a poor clerk who lived above his means and on whom, reputedly, Dickens was to base Mr Micawber.   In 1817, the family moved to Chatham in Kent. His childhood in the country was happy, though there was little money for education. The young Dickens, though frail, enjoyed reading, play-acting, singing and recitation.

In 1822, the family moved again to Camden, financial pressures increased and his happy childhood was ended when his father was imprisoned for debt. At twelve years old, young Charles was sent to work at a blacking factory for just six shillings a week. This experience left a bitter memory. He was determined never again to be short of money and his compassion for the impoverished and those abused by society probably originated from his experiences at this time. Not even his family knew of the experiences in the blacking factory until after his death. He kept 'the secret agony of my soul' to himself.

In 1827 he worked in the office of a firm of attorneys and later as a reporter of law proceedings and Parliamentary debates for *The Morning Chronicle* and, in 1833, *Mirror of Parliament.* His experience of the legal profession and of 'honourable' members of Parliament led to a contempt for their probity - both professions are satirised in later novels. However, Dickens developed a life-long passion for journalism.

Interest in a short story that had appeared in *Monthly Magazine* launched his writing career. He subsequently collected other stories and descriptive pieces that had appeared in other periodicals and re-published them as 'Sketches' under the pen name of 'Boz'. *Sketches by Boz* was published on his twenty-fourth birthday in 1836, the year he married Catherine Hogarth, daughter of the editor of the *Evening Chronicle*. These descriptive pieces focused on the lower middle classes, the level of society that Dickens knew so well. The book attracted a great deal of attention. An approach from a publisher led to the production of his first major literary work, *Pickwick Papers* (1836-7). This was published in instalments as were the rest of his novels. *Pickwick Papers* sold many copies and gave Dickens a large income and an admiring public.

His literary success was overshadowed in 1837 by the death of his much loved sister-in-law, Mary Hogarth, who lived with them. He never really recovered and her memory inspired Little Nell in *The Old Curiosity Shop*, Amy in *Little Dorrit* and Rose Maylie in *Oliver Twist* (1838). It was in *Nicholas Nickleby* (1838-9) that Dickens first began to expose social evils, particularly those of institutions. Working with great intensity (sometimes the novels overlapped), he next produced *The Old Curiosity Shop* (1840-1) and *Barnaby Rudge* (1841). With this novel he concluded the lighter novels in which he had shown a skill for comedy, melodrama and rich characterisation.

In 1842 he travelled to America, receiving a rapturous reception. He had always been a champion of causes and while there advocated international copyright and the abolition of slavery. His disillusionment with America is illustrated in *American Notes* (1842). This book caused offence, as did the bitter comments on American culture and society in *Martin Chuzzlewit* (1843-4), part of which is set in America, and which marked the beginning of his maturity as a writer. Prompted by the sight of the Ragged Schools, Dickens attempted to prick the social conscience by publishing two of his *Christmas Stories* just before Christmas in 1843 and 1844. These stories, which include *A Christmas Carol,* prompted the young Robert Louis Stevenson to write '....Oh what a jolly thing it is for a man to have written books like these and just filled people's hearts with pity'.

His next novels are more unified in theme and he displays a tighter control of structure and plot. The characters, too, have more psychological depth. *Dombey and Son* appeared in 1846-8, then *David Copperfield*. This is written in the first person as if autobiographical and Dickens drew on his childhood experiences. It was also Dickens's favourite novel.

Not only was Dickens prolific as a novelist but found time for his other interests and causes as well. In 1851 he formed the Guild of Art and Literature, an organisation putting on plays to raise money for needy authors and artists. As a journalist he founded and edited his own magazine, *Household Words*, started in 1850 and succeeded in 1859 by *All the Year Round* in which he published much of his later writing. *Bleak House* (1852-3) was followed by *Hard Times* (1854). Now wealthy as well as famous, he was able in 1856 to buy Gad's Hill, near Rochester in Kent.

As he got older, despite often poor health, he produced some of his best work. *Little Dorrit* (1855-7), *A Tale of Two Cities* (1859) and *Great Expectations* (1860-1). The latter, like *David Copperfield*, drew on his boyhood experiences around the marshes of the Kent countryside. *Our Mutual Friend* (1864-5) was the last complete novel. He died while writing *The Mystery of Edwin Drood*.

A few years before he died, Dickens had undertaken a series of readings of his work in America: an activity which gave him great pleasure. On his return, he embarked on a tour of the English provinces. It is thought by many that the punishing work schedule Dickens set himself as a writer and the great energy and intensity he put into his readings, his journalism and endless good causes finally killed him. He died at his home in Gad's Hill in 1870, leaving a fortune and, against his wishes, was buried with great ceremony in Westminster Abbey. Queen Victoria wrote in her diary, 'He is a very great loss .... He had a large loving mind and the strongest sympathy for the poorer classes'. To have written the novels would have been enough, but Dickens during his lifetime produced pamphlets such as *Sunday Under Three Heads* (1836 - opposed to Sabbath-breaking), *A Child's History of England* (1851-3), several short stories, pieces for *Household Words* (1860) and *All the Year Round* (1865), several comic plays and speeches and letters.

Outside literature and journalism, Dickens's main passion was for the theatre. He had been interested in it all his life, since being taken there as a child by his father. He had once considered becoming an actor and took part as an amateur in many productions. Many remarked that he looked and sounded like an actor with his flamboyant dress, long hair and gift for mimicry. It was while playing the lead in Wilkie Collins's *The Frozen Deep* in 1857 that he met the young actress Ellen Ternan who was to become his mistress. He wrote plays and organised festivals, but in later years reserved his energies for dramatic readings - or rather dramatic performances, for he involved himself totally with the characters. The surviving prompt copies' margin notes indicate that they were remarkably elaborate performances with visual and vocal effects. They were enormously popular and Dickens enjoyed reducing the audience to laughter or tears. A contemporary reviewer remarked, 'Mr Dickens is the greatest reader of the greatest writer of the age'.

During his lifetime, Dickens was considered to be the greatest living writer, widely read both in Britain and America. He held his public spellbound with the cliff-hanger endings of his serialisations, rather like the modern soap-operas of today. New York crowds waited anxiously on the docks for news of Little Nell in the next instalment of *The Old Curiosity Shop*. His reputation has remained undimmed today and he holds an important place in English literature. The term 'Dickensian' has entered the language and immediately conjures up a favourite scene or character - there are many to choose from. The weaknesses of which the twentieth century reader is aware - sentimentality, sensationalism and weak depiction of some female characters - are typical of the age and are far outnumbered by his strengths as a novelist. He is a great storyteller and observer of life, particularly of nineteenth century London for which he felt an 'attraction of repulsion'. Rich detailed descriptions, whether of a feast (*A Christmas Carol*), of fog (*Bleak House*), of feelings (particularly those of a child, based on his own experience in *Great Expectations* and *David Copperfield*) are important features of his work. His novels are crowded with memorable characters. Even the minor characters are individualised by physical or vocal eccentricities and the wealth of dialogue is a rich source of humour, adding vitality to the narrative. Characters' names, too, are often chosen for humour or for satire. Dickens's appeal as a writer is universal, evidenced by the way each new television, film or stage adaptation of his work can delight a new generation.

EMILY DICKINSON (1830-1886)

American poet

The daughter of an eminent lawyer and congressman, Edward Dickinson, she was born in Amherst, Massachussets where she lived all her life. She was educated at Amherst Academy and Mount Holyoake Female Seminary.

At first, she led a normal social life as the daughter of a prominent citizen. In her late 20s she withdrew from society and by the age of 30 had become a total recluse in her father's house, receiving very few visitors and dressing all in white. However, she regularly maintained correspondence with a select group of friends - among them Helen Hunt Jackson, the novelist.

Dickinson never married, though she had a series of intellectual relationships with men. The first of these was with Benjamin F. Newton, a law student who encouraged her poetry. When he died young she turned for religious guidance to the Revd. Charles Wadsworth, her 'dearest earthly friend', with whom she also maintained a correspondence. It was his departure for San Francisco in 1862 that saw her withdraw from society and occupy herself in writing. Although she had been writing from an early age, her most intensely creative period was in her late 20s and early 30s. She sent some of her poems to the author and critic Thomas Wentworth Higginson. This began a long correspondence between them (they only met twice) with Higginson becoming a kind of mentor, encouraging her to write, yet not fully recognising her genius.

She failed to get any of her work published. Publication, in her rather puritanical view, formed no part of a poet's business. She kept her efforts secret from her family, showing them to only a few close friends. She sometimes included poems in her letters to Hunt Jackson and another male friend, Samuel Bowles. Only seven - out of two thousand - poems were published in her lifetime. Some of these appeared in the *Springfield Republican*, a paper edited by Bowles, but they did so anonymously, substantially edited and were printed without her consent.

The bulk of her work was discovered only after her death in 1886. Her sister Lavinia found over a thousand poems in one room alone, bound together in neat home-made packets. Some had been carefully revised, others just jotted down on scraps of paper. The first published volume of her poetry was edited by Higginson and Mabel L. Todd in 1890 and 1891. Uncertain of their reception, the editors changed many of the original rhymes, metres and grammatical constructions.

As recognition for her talent grew, other poems and letters were published, restoring the original presentation and punctuation which had at first baffled her editors. *Bolts of Melody: New Poems of Emily Dickinson* (1945), edited by Todd and her daughter, was considered a breakthrough. It was more faithful to Dickinson's original texts than previous volumes and included many poems her relatives had suppressed. In 1955 Thomas H. Johnson prepared *The Poems of Emily Dickinson* containing all 1,775 known poems and this is accepted as the authoritative edition. *The Letters of Emily Dickinson* (1958), edited by Johnson and Theodora Ward, contains her enormous correspondence.

Emily Dickinson is now regarded as one of the most innovative of nineteenth century American poets and her work has influenced later writers. Her highly individual style, which was considered eccentric at first, included technical irregularities such as the use of dashes, capitals, ungrammatical phrasing, broken metres and strange rhymes. The simple forms (often two or four line stanzas), aphoristic wit, cryptic and often elliptical phrasing appear deceptively simple yet the tone is often complex. She referred to herself as 'The Queen of Calvary' and often expressed intense inner torment in images of violence, both of the natural and human kind: volcanoes, shipwrecks, storms, funerals. Emotions often conflict, such as pleasure and fear, reverence and rebellion. Despite her puritanical upbringing, religious doubt tormented her.

Much has been written by scholars and critics on the obvious break with convention displayed in Emily Dickinson's poetry. Time has seen opinions shift from regarding her as a naïve, eccentric poet not knowing her art, to a skilled and aesthetic artist.

DOUGLAS DUNN (born 1942)

British poet

Born in Renfrewshire, Scotland, the son of a factory worker. Educated in Scotland and at the University of Hull. He trained as a librarian and worked as such for ten years, for a time (1966-71) being employed as assistant to Philip Larkin. His poetry led to writers' residences and creative writing fellowships at various universities - Hull, Dundee and New England, Australia. He is now a Professor at the University of St. Andrew's.

While working in the library at Hull he produced *Terry Street* (1969), a series of striking poems about life in working class Hull. Some of these had already appeared in *The Times Literary Supplement* and *The New Statesman*. During the 1970s and 80s several more collections appeared which dealt with a more varied subject matter, among them *The Happier Life* (1972), *Love or Nothing* (1974), *Barbarian* (1979) and *St. Kilda's Parliament* (1981). The moving *Elegies* (1985) was written for his artist wife, Lesley, who died of cancer. This won him the Whitbread Book of the Year Award. The two most recent collections are *Northlight* (1988) and *Dante's Drum Kit* (1993).

Two of Dunn's main themes are his observations of the working class people of Hull and his memories of the slightly more respectable working class of his Scottish boyhood. With the first, the characters he describes are colourful and lively - but he sees them almost as an outsider, through a window. With the second, there is also a feeling of exile, both from childhood and his native Scotland. This is emphasised by a switch from the past to the present tense, and from the viewpoint of a child to that of an adult - especially when dealing with social envy and the awareness of class. Dunn uses down-to-earth language, in accordance with his subject matter. The poems rarely rhyme but often end with an epigrammatic statement making a final point or creating a poignant image. There are similarities with Larkin, who was an influence on his work.

He writes about himself in *Under the Influence: Douglas Dunn on Philip Larkin* (1987). He acknowledges the bleak landscape of the poems and the documentary of everyday provincial life. He discusses the poet as observer and outsider, but moves beyond this. Dunn has edited poetry collections and published a collection of short stories, *Secret Villages* (1985). He has also written radio and TV plays, most recently his televised poem, *Dressed to Kill* (1994). He has remarried (another artist), and has two children.

'His poems demonstrate the virtues of the very best photographs: they focus on a small, clearly defined subject and present it with clarity and emphasis'.

UMBERTO ECO (born 1932)

Italian novelist, critic and semiologist

Born Alessandria, Piedmont in Italy. He was educated at the University of Turin where he studied philosophy. He taught at that university (1956-67) and in 1971 became Professor of Semiotics (the study of signs) at the University of Bologna. He first established his reputation as a writer with books on semiotics, on which he is an authority. He is also a philosopher, historian, literary critic and aesthetician. His more academic publications include *The Absent Structure* (1968), *The Definition of Art* (1968), *The Form of Content* (1971), *A Theory of Semiotics* (1975) and *Semiotics and the Philosophy of Language* (1984).

Eco has made a prolonged study of the middle ages for which he has a 'taste and passion'. This revealed itself in his first (and best known) novel, a historical thriller, *The Name of the Rose* (1984). This made him a best selling author. Set in a medieval monastery, a crime is investigated by the English Franciscan, Brother William of Baskerville - the name of his 'detective' acknowledging the influence of Sir Arthur Conan Doyle and the Sherlock Holmes stories. *The Name of the Rose* was made into a successful film in 1987. *Reflections on The Name of the Rose* appeared in 1985, followed in 1989 by his second novel, *Foucault's Pendulum*, which is full of linguistic and theological puzzles.

Recent books have been *Misreadings* (1993), *How to Travel with a Salmon* (1994), and his latest novel, *The Island of the Day Before* (1995) which is set in the seventeenth century and is a seafaring adventure full of romance and suspense. Working in collaboration with Eugenio Carmi, Eco has written two books for children, *The Bomb and the General* (1989) and *The Three Astronauts* (1989). Eco writes a regular column in *L'Espresso* and contributes to a number of international periodicals including the *Times Literary Supplement*. He has made broadcasts on radio and television since the mid 1950s. *The Name of the Rose* earned him many awards and an Honorary Citizenship. Readers world wide delight in the way Eco draws on elements from philosophy, history, politics, cosmology, legend, theology, puns and puzzles and weaves them skilfully together into a thrilling plot that is mixed with intrigue and good humour.

T. S. (Thomas Stearns) ELIOT (1888-1965)

American-born British poet, critic and dramatist

Born in St. Louis, Missouri and educated at Harvard, the Sorbonne and Merton College Oxford. At Harvard, reading philosophy, he had already started writing poetry. He developed an aversion to Romanticism and admired Dante and the French symbolists, who would later influence his poetry. He taught at Highgate School, worked during the war for Lloyd's Bank and from 1917 was assistant editor for *The Egoist.*

In 1915 he came to live in England and married Vivien Haigh-Wood, whose highly strung and possessive nature would later cause him embarrassment and distress. In the same year, due to the influence of fellow American Ezra Pound, he had published his first important long poem, *The Love Song of J. Alfred Prufrock* in *Poetry* magazine. In 1917 it appeared again in his first volume, *Prufrock and Other Observations.* This was followed by *Poems* in 1919. The bleakness of his poems, their everyday imagery, fragmented verse and tone of despair showed clearly the break from Romanticism. Ezra Pound was helpful in editing Eliot's next and greatest poem, *The Waste Land* (1922), and it is to him that the poem is dedicated. It contained similarities of subject matter and style to his earlier work but it showed a complete break with tradition.

Eliot became the leader of a literary avant-garde, the voice of a disillusioned generation. *The Waste Land* was criticised for being too obscure - making use of over thirty literary allusions and six other languages - but it was also acknowledged as a major work for its originality and brilliant free verse style. It created much enthusiasm for Eliot's poetry.

In 1922 Eliot became editor of a new quarterly review, *The Criterion.* This became the most influential literary journal of the time. In 1925 he published his next volume of poetry, *Poems 1909-1925,* which includes *The Hollow Men.* This takes up the mood of frustration and despair of *The Waste Land* but is expressed in a plainer (and in some places liturgical) style which foreshadows the later poems. In 1927 Eliot became a British citizen and at the same time converted publicly to the Church of England. This shocked many of his contemporaries as they had considered him as agnostic in religion as he had been reactionary in literary style. He declared in the Introduction to *For Lancelot Andrewes* (1928), the year in which he became naturalised, that he was, 'classicist in literature, royalist in politics and Anglo-Catholic in religion'. His subsequent poetry deals more with matters of religious faith, devotion replacing disrespect, intensity replacing 'irony'. This change can be seen most notably in *Ash Wednesday,* a poem about the struggle for faith, and *The Journey of the Magi,* two well known poems that appeared in *Collected Poems 1909-1935* (1936).

In 1932 Eliot returned to America for the first time to lecture at Harvard and finally broke from his unhappy marriage. In 1943 he published *Four Quartets,* comprising *Burnt Norton, East Coker, The Dry Salvages* and *Little Gidding.* This is a poetic consideration of time and place. The *Collected Poems* (1909-62) were published in 1963.

Eliot also wrote several verse dramas in an attempt to revive the form, using a form of blank verse and natural speech patterns. The first of these, *The Rock* (1934), a verse pageant, asserts allegiance to the 'rock' of the Church. *Murder in the Cathedral* (1935), written to be performed in Canterbury Cathedral, dramatises the martyrdom of St Thomas Becket with the moral that only in religion can men find salvation.

Later verse plays, many of which have been presented on the London stage, are *The Family Reunion* (1939), *The Cocktail Party* (1950), *The Confidential Clerk* (1954) and *The Elder Statesman* (1959).

Eliot was also a major literary critic. His first volume of critical essays was *The Sacred Wood: Essays on Poetry and Criticism* (1920). This and *Towards the Definition of Culture* (1948) were both influential in the teaching of English Literature. As a literary critic his writings helped influence literary taste and revive interest, particularly in the Metaphysical poets and Elizabethan and Jacobean dramatists. Other volumes of criticism include *For Lancelot Andrewes* (1928), reflecting his Anglo-Catholic interests, *The Use of Poetry and the Use of Criticism* (1933), based on his Harvard lectures, *After Strange Gods* (1943) based on lectures given at the University of Virginia, *Notes Towards the Definition of Culture* (1948), *On Poetry and Poets* (1957) and *To Criticise the Critic* (1965). A volume of selected prose appeared in 1975. Eliot also produced *Old Possum's Book of Practical Cats* (1939), a children's classic on which Sir Andrew Lloyd-Webber based his musical, *Cats.* Eliot remarried in 1957 and towards the end of his life became something of a celebrity. *Time* magazine ran a feature on him in 1950. He won the Nobel Prize and the Order of Merit in the same year, 1948, and died in England in 1965. He is buried at East Coker, the village in Somerset from which his ancestors emigrated in the seventeenth century.

As a poet Eliot extended the range and means of expression in poetry and influenced a whole generation. His criticism, seen in relation to his own poetry, is revealing. In *The Sacred Wood* he declared, 'The only way of expressing emotion in the form of art is by finding an 'objective correlative', in other words, a set of objects, a situation, a chain of events, which shall be the formula of that particular emotion.' In *Tradition and the Individual Talent* (another essay from *The Sacred Wood*) he states, 'Poetry is not a turning loose of emotion but an escape from emotion, it is not the expression of personality, but an escape from personality'.

JAMES FENTON (born 1949)

British born poet and journalist

Born in Lincoln and educated at Repton School and Magdalen College, Oxford. He worked as a journalist both in England and abroad - in Germany in the 1970s and the Far East (including Vietnam) in the 1980s. He later became theatre critic for *The Sunday Times* and chief literary critic of *The Times*. He has also been responsible for the *Arts Poetica* column in *The Independent on Sunday*.

His first volume of poems, *Terminal Moraine* (1972), won the Eric Gregory Award. He used the proceeds to fund a trip to Cambodia to report on the Vietnam war for *The New Statesman*. Other publications include *A Vacant Possession* (1978) and *A German Requiem* (1980). *The Memory of War* (1982) contains poems based on his experiences as a war correspondent in Cambodia. This volume attracted considerable critical acclaim.

Fenton is regarded as an intellectual, writing mainly political, satirical poems that have the reticent tone of a man who has seen and experienced much. His poems display an objectivity, focusing on the outside world rather than internal feelings. In this respect he has been compared to W.H. Auden who let factual material evoke poetry. Fenton possesses, like Auden, wit and intellectual skill. The influence of Auden is apparent in the lyrics of two poems, *Dead Soldiers* and *Nothing*. Similarities have also been found to the new English 'narrative' poets and to poets of the 'Martian' school. These were a group of poets in the late 70s, led by Craig Raine, who presented familiar objects in unfamiliar ways. James Fenton coined the name 'Martian' for them himself and, like these poets, he sees the ordinary world as a strange and alien place. He does not, however, indulge in their extravagant use of simile or metaphor. Fenton has built up a reputation on the strength of a very small output of varied material - just over 100 pages between 1968 and 1983 - both light and more weighty verse.

Other publications include *Children in Exile* (1983), *Partingtime Hall*, satirical poems in collaboration with poet John Fuller (1987) and *Manila Envelope* (1989). He has adapted two plays and made a television documentary on *Burton: A Portrait of a Superstar* (1983). He was made a Fellow of the Royal Society of Literature in 1983 and Professor of Poetry at Oxford in 1994. He now lives in Oxford, continues to write for *The Independent* and his new volume of poetry *Out of Danger* contains lyrical poems as well as those on war and politics.

'A parsimonious brilliance … is its own reward' observed contemporary poet John Mole.

F. (Francis) SCOTT FITZGERALD (1896-1940)

American novelist and short story writer

Born at St. Paul, Minnesota, to a family of good breeding but very little money. His mother's family, who were of Irish descent, paid for his education. At Princeton he found diversion in sporting, theatrical and literary activities. He joined the army in 1917. Disappointed not to be sent overseas, he was stationed at Alabama. Here he first met the beautiful, talented but unstable Zelda Sayre, though at the time he did not have enough money to marry her. On his discharge Fitzgerald worked as an advertising copywriter in New York, trying unsuccessfully to become a journalist.

His first novel, *This Side of Paradise* was published in 1920. This autobiographical story was hailed as a great success for the way in which Fitzgerald had caught the mood of his generation. He was able to marry Zelda, and, also in 1920, wrote the first collection of short stories, *Flappers and Philosophers*. He and Zelda began to travel, living extravagantly in Europe and the USA. A second novel, *The Beautiful and Damned* was published in 1922. However, Fitzgerald still owed money to his publisher and collected together a number of short stories, most of which had first appeared in fashionable periodicals like *Vanity Fair, Saturday Evening Post* and *The Smart Set.* These were published as *Tales of the Jazz Age* (1922). The collection included the story, *The Diamond as Big as the Ritz,* which became well known. It was the first time the phrase 'the Jazz Age' had been used. Fitzgerald's phrase summed up the wild, spontaneous and rebellious spirit of young affluent America in the 1920s, represented by its music.

The glamorous Fitzgeralds rented a house at Great Neck, Long Island, but his attempt at playwriting, *The Vegetable* (1923), proved to be a flop and he was left heavily in debt. In 1924 they moved to St. Raphael in France. Fitzgerald took to drinking again - he was prone to alcoholism - and was devastated when he discovered his wife was having an affair. In 1925 his finest novel, *The Great Gatsby*, was published. It has been filmed twice, in 1949 and in 1974. Against the background of the glamorous high society he knew so well, it is the definitive Jazz Age novel. In the character of Jay Gatsby there is much of himself. *The Great Gatsby* met with great critical acclaim but commercially was not a success.

The summer of 1925 Fitzgerald described as one of '1000 parties and no work'. He met and helped Ernest Hemingway publish his novel and, forced by his financial circumstances, in 1927 made the first of his forays into Hollywood scriptwriting. In 1930 Zelda suffered a breakdown, the start of the schizophrenia that was later to hospitalise her. *Tender is the Night* (1934) is based on Fitzgerald's own experiences of his wife's mental illness. With its Riviera setting and characters drawn from the idle, rich society it was not received sympathetically during the Depression. Disappointed, Fitzgerald revised it repeatedly. He was financially and emotionally drained by his wife's now permanent hospitalisation and his own ill health from alcoholism and tuberculosis.

More short stories, *Taps at Reveille,* appeared in 1935. In 1937 he returned to Hollywood to become a scriptwriter with MGM. It was there that he met Sheilah Graham, the newspaper columnist, and their affair lasted until his death. Scriptwriting proved of limited success for Fitzgerald and he was eventually fired because of his drinking. Desperate, he turned back to writing novels and his last unfinished work, *The Last Tycoon* (1941), again drawing upon his own experiences in Hollywood, was published posthumously. During his last months he returned to writing short stories and these have been collected and published in *The Pat Hobby Stories* (1962). His editor said they represented, 'his last word from his last home, for much of what he felt about Hollywood and about himself permeated those stories'. During the 30s he had begun a series of touching pieces which chronicled his own decline, 'ten years this side of forty-nine, I suddenly realised that I had prematurely cracked'. These were posthumously collected and edited by his friend Edmund Wilson in *The Crack Up* (1945). In 1940 Fitzgerald died of a heart attack, just before his 45th birthday. Zelda died in 1948 and was buried beside him.

Fitzgerald was not only the most eloquent chronicler in his stories and novels of 'the Jazz Age' in America but, like his hero in *The Great Gatsby*, he was very much the embodiment of it - rich, handsome, athletic and talented. He not only wrote about glamorous high society, but was himself at its centre. His attitude towards this society is ambivalent, attracted by its charisma yet aware of its falseness. His stories are moralistic fables (particularly in *The Great Gatsby*, where the character of Nick comments as an 'outsider'). At the time of his death Fitzgerald, burnt out by alcoholism, illness and bankruptcy was considered a forgotten figure of the 20s. Posterity has proved him to be one of America's greatest twentieth century writers.

E. M. (Edward Morgan) FORSTER (1879-1970)

British novelist, short story writer, essayist and critic

Born in London, the son of a cultured family. His father died early and Forster was dominated by his widowed mother and his aunts. He was educated at Tonbridge (which he hated) and King's College, Cambridge (which he loved). In 1901 he was elected to the Apostles, an elite discussion society, through which he met members of the Bloomsbury Group. After graduating, he travelled widely in Greece and Italy and on his return contributed to *The Independent Review,* a liberal publication. He wrote his first short story, *The Story of Panic,* in 1904. In 1905 he went to Germany as tutor to the Countess von Arnim's children.

Forster wrote only six novels. Though his output is small, the quality of these novels established him as one of the foremost writers of the period. *Where Angels Fear to Tread* was published in 1905 and the following year he travelled back to Italy, where the novel is set, to lecture on Italian art and history. In that year he also became tutor and close friend of the Indian Moslem, Syed Ross Masood. *The Longest Journey* (1907) was followed by *A Room with a View* (1908) which, like the first novel, draws upon his experiences in Italy. Both are delicately handled social comedies which deal with serious themes and contrast the cultures of the repressed, hypocritical English with that of the emotional openness of the Southern European.

Next came his two masterpieces. *Howards End* (1910) established his reputation and *A Passage to India* (1924) was the last, and most acclaimed, novel published during his lifetime. Both deal with misunderstandings in relationships, between class and individuals in the one case and between races in the other - the clashes and prejudices between the British and Indians under the British Raj. Forster had made a first excursion to India in 1912, when he developed a loathing for Imperialism, and a second in 1921, returning as a private secretary to a maharajah. Depressed by the outbreak of war, he had gone to Egypt in 1915 to work for the International Red Cross. In Alexandria he met the Greek poet, Cavafy, whose work he introduced in England through translation.

As well as novels, Forster wrote three collections of short stories *The Celestial Omnibus* (1911), *The Story of the Siren* (1920) and *The Eternal Moment* (1928) and two critical works, *Aspects of the Novel* (1927) and *Abinger Harvest* (1936). He also wrote biographies. His miscellaneous collection of essays, lectures and talks on political and artistic themes were published in 1951 under the title, *Two Cheers for Democracy*. These essays are important for understanding his point of view. Basically Forster was a moralist, concerned for individual liberty. He advocated tolerance, culture and civilisation, and was opposed to barbarity and provincialism. He spoke out against racial prejudice, penal reform and freedom of expression. He took a firm stand against censorship by becoming actively involved with PEN, an international society of poets, editors, essayists and novelists, established to provide international goodwill and freedom of expression for writers. He was a witness for the defence during the trial of *Lady Chatterley's Lover* and he became the first President of the National Council for Civil Liberties. He was made an Honorary Fellow of King's College, Cambridge and from 1946 made the college his home. In 1951 he collaborated with Benjamin Britten on the libretto for his opera, *Billy Budd,* and in 1953 published *The Hill of Devi*, recalling his second visit to India.

He refused a knighthood in 1949 but accepted the Companion of Honour in 1953. In 1969 he was awarded the Order of Merit. *Maurice* (1971), his last novel, concerned with a young gentleman's acceptance of his homosexuality, was published posthumously, at Forster's request. The same is true of a collection of earlier short stories with a similar homosexual theme, *The Life to Come*.

All Forster's novels concern themselves with emotional restraint, a quality he saw as typical of the English race -

but also of the Edwardian age where social manners often replaced human contact even within families. His urge to 'only connect' is a phrase that has become a cliché. His stories often deal with the conflict between instinct and convention. He was a great storyteller but his plots are not always traditionally constructed. His ability to create complex characters and represent on paper their unconscious thoughts marks him out as a modern writer. He writes with precision and with a sometimes ironic detachment. His descriptive powers bring vividly alive the environments of his novels: the presence of India in *A Passage to India* has not been equalled. An intensely private intellectual, Forster lived frugally in his later years, despite his considerable wealth, although he was often generous to friends.

After 1942 he decided to publish no more novels. He wrote, 'I had been accustomed to write about the old-fashioned world with its homes and family lives and comparative peace. All that went, and though I can think about the new world, I cannot put it into fiction'. Posthumously his reputation has been enhanced by a number of successful film adaptations of his novels in the 1980s and 1990s.

ROY (Broadbent) FULLER (1912-1991)

British poet and novelist

Born at Failsworth, Lancashire. He was educated at Blackpool High School before qualifying as a solicitor in 1934. He enjoyed success in both his business and his literary career.

He first came to attention as a poet during the Second World War, when serving in the Royal Navy (1941-1946), most of the time in the Fleet Air Arm, attaining the rank of lieutenant. During the 1930s he contributed to left-wing literary magazines, including *New Verse*, and his first volume, *Poems* (1939), reveals the influences of W.H. Auden and Stephen Spender. His work was first published in *Penguin New Writing* and *The Listener*. He became a close friend of

J.R. Ackerley and a regular contributor of reviews to the BBC magazine for which Ackerley was literary editor. After the war he specialised in legal work relating to building societies. He became chairman of the building societies legal advice panel (1958-69) and subsequently a director. *Image of a Society*, often considered his best novel, is based on his experience at the Woolwich. In later life he served as chairman of the Arts Council as well as being a governor of the BBC. From 1968-1973 Fuller was Professor of Poetry at Oxford and two volumes of his Oxford lectures were published.

Collected Poems 1936-61 was published in 1962 and *New Poems* won the Duff Cooper Memorial Prize in 1968. *Off Course* (1969), *From the Joke Shop* (1975), *The Reign of Sparrows* (1980), *New and Collected Poems 1934-1984, Last Poems* (1993). Fuller's novels include *Image of a Society* (1956), *The Ruined Boys* (1959), *The Father's Comedy* (1961), *My Child, My Sister* (1965) and *The Carnal Island* (1970). For children he has written *Savage Gold* (1946), *With My Little Eye* (1948), *Catspaw* (1966), *Seen Grandpa Lately?* (1972), *Poor Roy* (1977), *The Other Planet* (1979) and *Upright Downfall* (1983). His autobiography was published in three volumes - *Souvenirs* (1980), *Vamp Till Ready* (1982) and *Home and Dry* (1984). Fuller married in the 1930s and his only son is the poet, novelist and Oxford don, John Fuller. Roy Fuller was awarded the CBE in 1970.

STELLA GIBBONS (1902-1989)

British novelist, poet and journalist

Born in London, the eldest of three children of a doctor. She did not go to school at first but was educated at home by a governess. As a form of escape from an unhappy childhood, she read books set in exotic places and told stories to her younger brothers. Her story-telling continued when she eventually went to school at 13. At the North London Collegiate College, the other girls enjoyed her 'school' stories.

A course in journalism followed at University College, London.

The next ten years were spent in Fleet Street in a variety of jobs: as a reporter, literary and drama critic and fashion writer. She later said that reviewing novels for the *Lady* sharpened her gift for satire. Throughout this period she continued to write poetry and short stories. Her first volume of poetry, *The Mountain Beast,* was published in 1930, containing nature and pastoral poems. She turned sharply against such fashion with her first and only major novel *Cold Comfort Farm* (1932). This satirises the pretensions of Fleet Street and is a witty parody of the 'primitive' rural novel of such writers as Mary Webb, Sheila Kaye-Smith, Hardy and D.H. Lawrence. Her witty parody won her instant fame and the Femina Vie Heureuse Prize. The following year, 1933, she married Allan Bourne Webb, an actor and opera singer by whom she had a daughter. There was a musical version of *Cold Comfort Farm* in 1965, its title - *Something Nasty in the Woodshed* - taken from the novel's most quoted line. In 1968 and 1995, television adaptations were made.

Gibbons never achieved the same success with her following works, which suffered by comparison - despite attempts to revive interest with two collections of short stories, *Christmas at Cold Comfort Farm* (1940) and *Conference at Cold Comfort Farm* (1949). In all she wrote twenty-five novels, four volumes of poetry and three collections of short stories over the next forty years, though she saw herself as a poet rather than a novelist. Many of her later novels are set in literary North London, an area she knew well, and contain sharp social observations. These witty comedies of manners met with some success but none to equal that of *Cold Comfort Farm.* Her other publications include *The Priestess and other Poems* (1924), *The Lowland Venus and Other Poems* (1938), *Collected Poems* (1950), *Bassett* (1934), *Nightingale Wood* (1938), *The Bachelor* (1944), *The Pink Front Door* (1959), *The Charmer* (1965), *Starlight* (1967), *The Snow Woman* (1969) and *The Woods in Winter* (1970). She was elected fellow of the Royal

Society of Literature in 1950 and was writing up until the time she died, aged 87.

GRAHAM GREENE (1904-1991)

British writer of novels, plays and non-fiction

Born at Berkhamsted and educated at the school there, where his father was headmaster, and at Balliol College, Oxford. He became a journalist, joining the staff of *The Times*, which he left to pursue a writing career.

During World War II Greene worked in the Foreign Office and was an MI6 agent. His wide travels, particularly into dangerous and politically unstable parts of the world, provided the settings for later novels. His first novel, *The Man Within,* appeared in 1929 and he quickly became one of the most discussed contemporary writers. He divided his fictional works into two categories: 'entertainments' and 'novels'. As there is no clear line of demarcation, the definitions are not taken too seriously.

The 'entertainments' include his early novels, *The Man Within* (1929), *Stamboul Train* (1932), *A Gun for Sale* (1936), *Brighton Rock* (1938), *The Ministry of Fear* (1943) and *The Confidential Agent* (1939). Influenced by the action films of the time, and the style of writer John Buchan (as Greene acknowledged), these thrillers are distinguished by fugitive heroes and shadowy backgrounds where good opposes evil. The 'entertainments' culminated in Greene's own atmospheric film scripts, of which the best, directed by Carol Reed was *The Third Man* (1950). The thrillers and later comedies such as *Our Man in Havana* (1958), *Travels with my Aunt* (1969) and *Monsignor Quixote* (1988) were less important (in Greene's own estimation) than the more serious novels of his later period: *The Power and the Glory* (1940), *The Heart of the Matter*

(1948), *The End of the Affair* (1951), *The Quiet American* (1955) and *A Burnt Out Case* (1961).

Graham Greene has defined a novelist's function as 'to try to engage people's sympathy for characters who are outside the official range of sympathy'. After his conversion to Catholicism in 1926, Greene's religious views greatly influenced his work. Though he remained a doubtful Catholic throughout his life, his novels, notably *Brighton Rock* and *The Heart of the Matter*, frequently exploit religious conflicts. The 'characters' he talked of tended to be shabby souls, tormented by their own moral failure, veering towards damnation but not beyond salvation and God's forgiveness. Religion often goes hand in hand with crime or degeneracy in these 'Catholic' novels and the vision of the world they depict is often gloomy. Other novels include *The Comedians* (1966), *A Sort of Life* (1971), *The Honorary Consul* (1973, his personal favourite), *The Human Factor* (1978), *The Tenth Man* (1985) and *The Captain and the Enemy* (1988). As well as novels he has written several successful plays: *The Living Room* (1953), *The Potting Shed* (1957), *The Complaisant Lover* (1959) and *The Return of A.J. Raffles* (1975). He also produced short stories, criticism, film reviews, books for children and travel books. The latter describe journeys in Liberia (*Journey without Maps* 1936), Mexico (*The Lawless Roads* 1939) and Africa (*In Search of a Character: two African Journals,* 1961).

His collected essays appeared in 1969 and autobiographical works include *A Son of Life* (1971), *Ways of Escape* (1981) and *Getting to Know the General* (1984). He was made a Companion of Honour in 1966 and a Chevalier de la Legion d'Honneur in 1969 and given the Order of Merit in 1986.

Graham Greene was one of the most prolific and greatest of our modern novelists who achieved both critical and popular acclaim. He was a great storyteller whose characters are well drawn and whose settings evoke a strong atmosphere. A preoccupation with the personal, political and moral dilemmas of characters who are often second rate, tainted heroes set against exotic but deprived locations characterise his work.

PHOEBE HESKETH (born 1909)

British poet and journalist

Born in Preston, Lancashire, the daughter of a pioneer radiologist. She describes her family as, 'a world of maids, culture, riding and conformity that bred rebellion and eccentricity'. Educated at Preston High School, Dagfield Birkdale School and Cheltenham Ladies College, Phoebe Hesketh enjoyed poetry as a child. Her favourite collection was Robert Louis Stevenson's *A Child's Garden of Verses*. She began writing early, winning several competitions. In 1926 she left school to nurse her dying mother.

In 1931 she married Aubrey Hesketh and bore three children. She combined domestic life with her passion for horses, writing and reading. She began contributing articles to magazines and, in 1939, *Poems* was published. During the war years (1942-5) she edited the women's page of the *Bolton Evening News* and then worked as a freelance journalist.

She has published several volumes of poetry including *Lean Forward Spring* (1948), *No Time for Cowards* (1952), *Out of the Dark* (1954), *Between Wheels and Stars* (1956), *The Buttercup Children* (1958), *Prayer for Sun* (1966), *A Song of Sunlight* (for children 1974), *Preparing to Leave* (1977), *The Eighth Joy* (1980), *Over the Brook* (1986) and *Netting the Sun* (1989). She has given readings of her poems, many of which appeared in *Country Life* magazine and were subsequently anthologised as *The Fox*. As well as articles in journals, she has written plays and documentaries for radio including, *One Pair of Eyes*.

Hesketh's published prose consists of *My Aunt Edith* (1966 - a biography of her father's suffragette sister, Edith Rigby), *Rivington: The Story of a Village* (1972 - dealing with the village where she and her family had lived for 40 years), and *What Can the Matter Be?* (1985 - an account of her growing up, also broadcast on radio). She has worked as a lecturer since 1967 and has twice won the Poetry Society Greenwood Prize (1948, 1966). She has been elected a Fellow of the Royal Society of Literature (1950) and been an active member of PEN, winning a first prize in an international poetry competition in 1988.

Phoebe Hesketh's poetry draws mainly on the stark country landscape of the North and the characters and animals that live there. The scenes and activities she describes are very much based on real people but they are not merely descriptive, using the moods of nature to reflect the human spirit. There is often a theme of searching, 'to find the unknown through the known'. She was influenced by the Romantics in her early work but came more to admire the American poets Robert Frost and Edward Thomas. Her later poetry is more philosophical and personal, using her experiences of bereavement (her son was drowned), age and loneliness - 'writing for me now is the process of stripping to the bone - with rare bursts of lyricism'. Her later poetry also touches on environmental issues when she sees 'devastation in the unsacred name/of silence mock the cratered human heart'.

MICHAEL HOLROYD (born 1935)

British author and biographer

Born in London and educated at Eton. He claims to have 'read literature' and gained his learning at Maidenhead Public Library. He is best known as a biographer. His first book was on Hugh Kingsmill (1964), followed by a two volume life of

Lytton Strachey: *The Unknown Years* (1967) and *The Years of Achievement* (1968). This was revised and reissued in one volume in 1971. The Strachey biography was much admired and led to a renewed interest in the Bloomsbury Group. Holroyd was also credited with reviving biography writing as an art form. His two other principal subjects have been Augustus John (1974-5, revised and reissued in one volume 1976) and George Bernard Shaw (1988-91).

Holroyd's essays and articles are collected under the title, *Unreceived Opinions* (1973). He has also edited several books: a selection of Kingsmill's work, *The Best of Hugh Kingsmill* (1970), *Lytton Strachey By Himself, The Art of Augustus John, The Genius of Shaw, The Shorter Strachey* and, with William Gerhardie, *God's Fifth Column, A Biography of the Age: 1890-1940.* Holroyd was chairman of the Society of Authors (1973-4), Chairman of the National Book League (1976-8) and Resident of the English branch of PEN from 1985-8 (an international association of poets, playwrights, editors, essayists and novelists founded in 1921 to promote co-operation between writers in the interests of literature and freedom of expression). He has also served on the Literature Panel of the Arts Council and lectured both in Britain and America. As well as contributing articles to newspapers and magazines, he has written scripts for television including *Aquarius* and *The South Bank Show.*

He received the CBE in 1989 and is married to the novelist Margaret Drabble. His revised biography of Lytton Strachey (1994) gave more focus to his relationship with the painter Dora Carrington and was the basis of the film, *Carrington,* starring Jonathan Pryce and Emma Thompson.

'His prose in this second version is as elegant as ever.
He is also one of the few biographers who has retained
a pronounced sense of humour.'

Peter Ackroyd in *The Times*
on the revised biography of Lytton Strachey

TED HUGHES (born 1930)

British poet

Born in Mytholmroyd, West Yorkshire, the son of a carpenter. Educated at Mexborough Grammar School and, after a spell of National Service, at Pembroke College, Cambridge.

The stories his father told him of the suffering and violence of World War I had a profound effect on him as did the bleak Yorkshire countryside. Shooting and fishing trips with his brother sparked a keen interest in wildlife and a sense of both the beauty and the cruelty of nature. He met the American poet Sylvia Plath at Cambridge and married her in 1956, later becoming a teacher. He has published many collections of verse. The first two established him as a major new talent and important poet of the post-war period. *The Hawk in the Rain* (1957) created something of an impact and won him a Guinness Poetry Award and Guggenheim Fellowship from 1959-60. *Lupercal* in 1960 won a Somerset Maugham Award and the Hawthornden Prize.

Sylvia Plath's suicide in 1963 had a stunning effect on him and for a while he published very little. *Wodwo* (1967) was followed by an extraordinary sequence of poems which contained the central symbol of a predatory crow, also to appear in later work. *Crow* (1970) received much acclaim but also shocked a great many by its violence.

In 1971 Hughes went to Iran and wrote *Orghast,* a verse drama for the director Peter Brook, much of which is in an invented language. Subsequent volumes include *Cave Birds* (1975), *Moortown* (1979), *Remains of Elmet* (1979 - a collection of verse with photographs of the landscapes of his youth in the Calder valley), *Under the North Star* (1981), *River* (1983 - again including photographs), *Season Songs* (1985) and *Flowers and Insects* (1986). His later poetry, less macabre and with a gentler tone, is, perhaps, less compelling. Despite his reputation as a 'violent' poet, Ted Hughes has written numerous poems, stories and plays for children, among them

Meet My Folks (1961), *Earth Owl and other Moon People* (1963), *How the Whale Became* (1963) and *The Iron Man* (1968). He has written two librettos for the composer Gordon Crosse and adapted Seneca's *Oedipus* (1968) for the National Theatre. He has published stories, written radio plays and edited numerous anthologies, notably *The Rattle Bag* (1982) with Seamus Heaney.

In 1977 Hughes was awarded the OBE and in 1984 succeeded John Betjeman as Poet Laureate. His Laureate poems are collected in *Rain-Charm for the Duchy* (1992) in which he dwells on the mythical idea of Englishness, a central theme in his *Shakespeare and the Goddess of Complete Being* (1992).

Some of the characteristics which distinguish Hughes from his contemporaries are the vivid and stark descriptions of his subjects, often the birds, beasts, countryside and weather of the natural world seen in the raw: harsh and violent, 'red in tooth and claw,' as he described it. He shows an extraordinary ability to identify with and become the creature he describes, sharing its feelings and experiences, celebrating in its nobility and predatory nature, recognising aspects of its nature that are shared by humans. The bird/animal is often presented as an alien to civilisation, the struggle for survival a recurring theme. The language is made forceful by exaggeration and striking use of metaphor.

Hughes's fondness for Yeats encouraged the use of folk tale and myth in many of the poems (*Wodwo*). Gerard Manley Hopkins and Dylan Thomas influenced the vigour and rhythm of his language, often used effectively to mirror the movement of different animals. Although seen by admirers as 'the most explosively individual poetic talent to appear in England since the war', Hughes is not without his critics. In answer to those who condemn the violence of the poems, he replied, 'My poems are not about violence but vitality'. It was important for him that his readers should experience that vital life force, intensified in moments of captivity, pain or death - to observe it, admire it and learn from it. British poetry had been dominated by the 'Movement'. They found Hughes too violent and unrestrained in his style, too self-indulgent - in contrast to their own writing, which was urbane and detached. Hughes was a key member of the 'New Poetry,' which came to prominence as a group in an anthology of that name edited by A. Alvarez in 1962. Alongside Thom Gunn he was the most representative of that period and has been much imitated since.

'The poems crackle with surplus energy. The words leap off the page to grapple or strike the reader'.

Keith Sagar in *The Art of Ted Hughes*

KERI HULME (born 1947)

New Zealand novelist, poet and short story writer

Born in Christchurch, she was educated at Canterbury University. She is of mixed descent, Maori (Kai Tahu, the South Island tribe), Scots (Orkneys) and English (Lancashire). In all her writing she draws extensively from her ancestral and cultural heritages, particularly the Maori. She rarely writes out of the context of her homeland, because, as she says, she is 'lucky enough to be a mongrel'.

She left home at 18 and had various jobs: postwoman, TV director, itinerant and seasonal worker. She became a full-time writer at 25. Since 1973 she has won many literary grants and awards in New Zealand. Her various poems and uncollected short stories have appeared in magazines - including *Hooks and Feelers*, which was adapted for television in 1984.

Her first volume of poetry, *The Silences Between (Moeraki conversations)* (1982), is partly written in Maori, partly in English. Her first novel, *The Bone People,* began as a short story and took twelve years to write. It won the New Zealand Book Award for fiction and the Pegasus Award for Maori

Literature before being published in Britain. Here, despite being the outsider, it won the Booker Prize in 1985. It is a mythical narrative that reflects on Maori legend and culture. It uses powerful images and dreams to personify aspects of the characters' thoughts that are a mix of Maori myth and Christian symbolism. She acknowledged the influence of Jung on this novel. It was much praised in New Zealand for the way the language reflects Maori phrases and idiom. This is a striking feature in the book which contributes to its vitality. It was also much discussed for the hybrid interpretation of contemporary New Zealand society - for Hulme the Maori are like the disabled in a fit society. The prose style is experimental and shifts in time and place. She makes use of fragmented dialogue and stream-of-consciousness narrative (narrative technique representing directly the characters' flow of feelings and thoughts). She has written, 'What I write is fantasy - solidly based in reality'. She also claims to write 'from a visual base and a gut base rather than sieving it through the mind'.

Since 1985 Hulme has been writer-in-residence at Canterbury University, New Zealand. She has also published a collection of short stories, *Te Kaihau: The Windeater* (1986), written during the previous ten years. They touch on similar themes to *The Bone People* but are more radically feminist. They are a good introduction to her work. She has also published two other collections of poetry, *Lost Possessions* (1985) and *Strands* (1992). She lives in Okarito Westland on New Zealand's South Island, supporting herself by writing, fishing and painting. She was a founder member of the Wellington Women's Gallery and exhibits regularly. Environmental and feminist issues and the Maori cultural identity, past and present, are central to her life and work.

'I have a grave suspicion that life is a vast joke: We are unwitting elements of the joke.'

'I write about people who are in pain because they can't see the joke, see the point of the joke.'

'I want to touch the raw nerves in New Zealand - the violence we largely cover up; the racism we don't acknowledge, the spoilation of land and sea - and explore why we (Maori) have developed a very curious type of humour .... which is a steel-sheathed nerve I want to hide inside'.

Keri Hulme on *The Bone People*

'In this novel, New Zealand's people, its heritage, and landscape are conjured up with uncanny poetry and perceptiveness.'

The Sunday Times

'Keri Hulme is a poet. The power and feeling for nature and the more mystical sides of a dwindling people, the Maoris, will make it a gem providing a whole new range of experience.'

The Daily Telegraph

GIUSEPPE TOMASI DI LAMPEDUSA (1896-1957)

Italian novelist

Born in Palermo, Sicily into an aristocratic family, the son of the Duke of Parma and grandson of the Prince of Lampedusa. Once rich, his family had lost much of their wealth and, after a period of wildness in his youth, di Lampedusa became a rather studious young man reading avidly in several languages.

Once his mother - the dominant influence in his life - died, he felt the freedom to write what was to be his one great novel, *Il Gattopardo* (1958), published in English as *The Leopard* (1960). The novel describes the decline of aristocratic society in Sicily following the island's annexation by Garibaldi during the unification of Italy in 1860. Nostalgia is mixed with aversion to the violence and decadence he describes during the political and social changes that inevitably followed. The novel was well received but later vilified by the Italian literary establishment. Now it is generally regarded as one of the greatest Italian novels of the twentieth century. It was made into a film by Visconti in 1963 starring Burt Lancaster.

PHILIP LARKIN (1922 - 85)

British poet

Philip Larkin was born in Coventry, the son of a local government official. He was educated at King Henry VIII School, Coventry and at St. John's College, Oxford. Here he became friends with Kingsley Amis and the poet John Wain. From 1943 he worked as a librarian in various university libraries and from 1955 was chief librarian at the Brynmor Jones Library, Hull University. He remained at the Brynmor Jones until his death, despite achieving fame as a poet.

His first collection of poems, *The North Ship*, was published in 1945. Although this was greatly admired, his reputation was built upon three 'mature' collections of poetry - *The Less Deceived* (1955); *The Whitsun Weddings* (1964) which won the Queens' Gold Medal for Poetry in 1965 and the Arts Council Prize; and *High Windows* (1974), which received more awards. He also published two novels, *Jill* (1946) and *A Girl in Winter* (1947) and a collection of essays on jazz; *All What Jazz?* (1970). He had been jazz critic of the *Daily Telegraph* from 1961 to 1971 and remained a life-long devotee.

From 1970-1 he was made Varsity Fellow of All Saints College, Oxford and while there worked on an anthology, *The Oxford Book of Twentieth Century English Verse* (1973), controversial because of his choices. *Required Writing: Miscellaneous Pieces* (1955-82) is a collection of critical essays and reviews. When John Betjeman died, Larkin was asked to accept the post of Poet Laureate but he declined, despite being worried about offending Mrs Thatcher, whom he greatly admired. He was made Companion of Honour in 1985, the year he died after surgery for cancer.

Posthumous publications include *Collected Poems* (1988) and *Selected Letters* (1982). Philip Larkin is considered one of the central figures of The Movement (also called 'New Liners' after these poets featured in an anthology called *New Lines* ed. Robert Conquest 1956), a group of writers in the mid 1950s who were first noticed and given their name by the literary editor of the *Spectator*, J.D. Scott. As well as Larkin, they included Kingsley Amis and John Wain (Larkin's contemporaries from Oxford), Donald Davie, D.J. Enright and Elizabeth Jennings. Their work was characterised by 'a return to a cool tone, tight form and intellectual backbone after some of the romantic excesses of the 1940s'. They had turned away from the obscurity of T.S. Eliot and the romanticism of Dylan Thomas and wrote about the ordinary, often in a sardonic tone. Honest expression of feeling is what they sought, writing in a direct, objective, sometimes pessimistic manner marked by irony and doubt. These features certainly appear in Larkin's poetry. His landscape is provincial urban life.

He wrote, 'Deprivation is for me what daffodils were to Wordsworth'. Everyday situations with all their banality is what interests him ('the sense that most of the time to most people nothing much happens' - Alan Bennett). He himself despised what he called 'high emotion' and believed that 'a poem's meaning should be communicated directly and often ends with an evaluation of an experience or event' - in a typically objective way as a detached observer. Kingsley Amis, who knew him well, said that some of Larkin's poems were by the man he knew, others by someone else. 'The I is always the eye. It is not always I' (Alan Bennett's observation from Amis's remark in 'Poetry in Motion').

A pessimistic attitude is present throughout the poems, though Larkin disagreed with this assessment. However negative his poems appear, one should never forget that the writing of them was a positive thing to do, he argued. Poetry from *The Less Deceived*, when The Movement began, appears darker and more bitter. Despite these features, common to poets of the group, Larkin has qualities that set him apart and indeed elevate him. His writing has a much wider range of subject matter and feeling, there are displays of tenderness along with the irony and underlying humour. To communicate directly, Larkin avoids the 'bookishness' he despised and adopts colloquial, often vulgar language, and contemporary speech rhythms. This engenders a familiarity, a bond with the reader, despite the poet's detachment.

The verse is very well constructed. Robert Lowell called him 'the most formally satisfying British poet of his time'. John Mortimer has summed up Larkin's particular qualities: 'his work is touching, ironic, unexpectedly tender, unsentimental and often sad'. Larkin, of course, was well-read and he admired and acknowledged the influence of other writers on him. In the new edition of *The North Ship* (1973), he described how he exchanged the influence of W.B. Yeats for that of Thomas Hardy, admiring his directness and honesty in expressing feelings. The pessimism too was probably influenced by Hardy. He admired Betjeman for writing 'comprehensive poems in a regular metre' and for his fascination with the 'variety of personality that is shown by men and women'.

Overall, Larkin's output was not great. Three slim volumes of mature verse - a mere 85 poems over a period of thirty years - but the high quality of what he did produce ranks him along with Ted Hughes as one of the two most important poets since the war. He is considered by some to be the finest poet of his generation - a generation whose voice and attitude he evokes so well.

D. H. (David Herbert) LAWRENCE (1885-1930)

British novelist and poet

Born in 1885 in the coal mining village of Eastwood, Nottinghamshire, the fourth child of Arthur, a miner, and

Lydia, an ex-schoolmistress. He was a delicate child, later to develop tuberculosis, and grew up in poverty.

Lawrence was very close to his mother and she made considerable sacrifices to enable him to gain an education at Nottingham High School and University. She was determined to keep him from the collieries. He became a school teacher and, encouraged by Ford Madox Ford and Edward Garnett, began to write. After his first novel, *The White Peacock* (1911) he gave up teaching for writing.

In 1912 his second novel *The Trespasser* was published. In 1913 *Love Poems and Others* was followed by *Sons and Lovers*, his first major novel in which he described the environment of his early years. During this period he eloped to Germany with Frieda Weekley - wife of his former tutor at Nottingham University and cousin of the German air ace, von Richthoffen. They married in London in July 1914 after Frieda's divorce.

The outbreak of World War I prevented the couple from returning to Europe and Lawrence began to make friends in literary and intellectual circles. *The Rainbow* was published in 1915 but was suppressed as obscene. German-born Frieda was treated with hostility and in 1916, when living in Cornwall, the Lawrences were at first ostracised and then evicted on the grounds of spying. However, he still managed to publish two more volumes of poetry - *Amores* (1916) and *Look, We Have Come Through* (1917) - and worked on *Women in Love* (privately printed in New York in 1920).

The Lost Girl (begun before the war) won the James Tait Black Memorial Prize in 1920; the only official honour Lawrence was to receive during his lifetime. *Aaron's Rod* followed in 1922, and in the same year he travelled to Ceylon, Australia and finally to America and Mexico. In 1922, while in Australia, he wrote *Kangaroo* and *Studies in Classic American Literature*. Lawrence's travels provided the inspiration for his writing but also had a damaging effect upon his weak constitution. His last major work, *Lady Chatterley's Lover*, was completed in 1926-28. It was privately printed in Florence and was finally published in unexpurgated editions in the

United States and England over thirty years later, after unsuccessful prosecutions for obscenity. In February 1930, Lawrence entered a sanitorium at Vence in France, suffering from tuberculosis, where he died on 2nd March.

Short stories include: *The Prussian Officer* (1914), *England, My England* (1922), *The Woman who Rode Away* (1928), complete edition in three volumes 1955.

Travel books: *Twilight in Italy* (1916), *Sea in Sardinia* (1921), *Mornings in Mexico* (1927), *Etruscan Places* (1932).

Poetry: *Birds, Beasts and Flowers* (1923), *Pansies* (1929), *Complete Poems,* (three volumes 1957).

Plays: *The Widowing of Mrs Holroyd* (1920), *Touch and Go* (1920), *David* (1927), *A Collier's Friday Night* (1965), *The Daughter-in-Law* (1967), *The Fight for Barbara* (1967).

C. S. (Clive Staples) LEWIS (1898 - 1963)

British novelist, critic and scholar

Born in Belfast, the son of a solicitor. He both read and wrote avidly as a child. He was sent away to a series of all-male schools on his mother's death, when he was only 10. It was at school he discovered mythology and lost Christianity. He was educated briefly at Malvern before winning a scholarship to University College, Oxford. His studies were interrupted by war service in France (1917-18) where, while convalescing after being wounded, he befriended Mrs Moore, the mother of a friend who had been killed. He shared a house in Oxford with Mrs Moore until her death in 1951, referring to her as 'mother'. After achieving a triple first at Oxford (as well as classics and philosophy he took a fourth year in English), he became Fellow and Tutor at Magdalen College, Oxford (1925-54). During this period he published his first book, *Dymer* (1926), using the pseudonym 'Clive

Hamilton.' He also cultivated the friendships of 'The Inklings' - a group of writers, including J. R. R. Tolkien, who met in his Oxford rooms over many years to discuss religion and literature and read aloud their own work. He was made a Professor of Medieval and Renaissance English at Cambridge in 1954.

His major writing began with *The Pilgrim's Regress* (1933), which recounts his conversion back to Christianity. Other academic publications include *The Allegory of Love* (1936 - a famous study on the medieval tradition of courtly love), *A Preface to Paradise Lost* (1942), *The Abolition of Man* (1943), *English Literature in the Sixteenth Century* (1954), *Studies in Words* (1960), *An Experiment in Criticism* (1961) and *The Discarded Image* (1963). Many of these books were based on his lectures. As well as scholarly books, he wrote three allegorical science-fiction novels which have a religious theme: *Out of the Silent Planet* (1938), *Perelandra* (1943) and *That Hideous Strength* (1945).

He is best remembered for a series of enchanting children's books, that have now become classics of children's literature. These are the seven *Narnia* books (1950-6), beginning with *The Lion, the Witch and the Wardrobe* and ending with *The Last Battle*. In these he uses myth and fairy-tale together with Christian parable. He achieved wide popularity not only with these stories but also during the war when he gave talks on the radio on Christianity (1952). Lewis wrote several books on Christian ethics, beginning with *The Problem of Pain* (1940) and including *Miracles* (1947), *Surprised by Joy* (1955 - a spiritual autobiography), *The Four Loves* (1960) and the very popular *Screwtape Letters* (1942) which examines Christianity from the point of view of the Devil and the nephew with whom he corresponds. *Till We Have Faces* (1956) is a sequel to *The Allegory of Love*.

In 1956, when he was in his late 50s he married Joy Gresham, an American divorcée. She died of cancer not long afterwards in 1960 and *A Grief Observed* (1961) is a moving account of her illness and death. Their relationship is the subject of William Nicholson's acclaimed play, *Shadowlands* (1989), which was made into an award-winning film starring Anthony Hopkins and Debra Winger.

(Frederick) LOUIS MacNEICE (1907-63)

British poet

Born in Belfast, the son of a rector who later became a bishop, MacNeice was educated at Marlborough and Merton College, Oxford. Here he published his first volume of poetry, *Blind Fireworks* (1929), and met with W.H. Auden, Stephen Spender and C. Day Lewis. Although he is associated with these poets and had socialist sympathies, MacNeice remained on the outside of the group, 'a radical but never a Marxist, a bohemian but fond of family life' (Alan Bennett). He was an agnostic in politics, as he was in religion.

After academic success at Oxford, gaining a double first, he became a lecturer in Classics for the next ten years, first at Birmingham University (1930-6) and then at Bedford College, London (1936-40). He published several volumes of poetry in the 1930s including *Poems* (1937), *The Earth Compels* (1938) and one of the best, *Autumn Journal* (1938), followed by *Autumn Sequel* in 1954. After a visit to Ireland he collaborated with W.H. Auden to write *Letters from Ireland* (1937) which combine verse and prose.

After visits to Spain and the USA (lecturing at Cornell University), he returned to England at the start of the war and in 1940 joined the features department of the BBC and became a writer/producer. His duties included overseas assignments. During this period he wrote plays for the stage and even more for the radio as well as features, including the much acclaimed *The Dark Tower* (1946).

After his first marriage ended, he married actress/singer Hedli Anderson in 1942. She was associated with the Group Theatre and had performed works by Auden and Benjamin Britten.

MacNeice's *Collected Poems 1925-1948* were published in 1949. There was a decline in his work after the war but by the late 1950s his career rose again. His later poems have an underlying note of pessimism, a sense of impermanence evident in *Solstices* (1961). He resigned from the BBC in 1961 to concentrate on his own work, but died not long afterwards. The cause of death was pneumonia which followed a chill resulting from working down a pothole for a BBC programme. As well as his poetry, MacNeice wrote one novel, *Roundabout Way* (1932), two children's stories, critical works - the most notable being *The Poetry of W.B. Yeats* (1941) - and acclaimed verse translations (while a lecturer in Classics) of *The Agamemnon of Aeschylus* (1936) and *Goethe's Faust* (1951). Posthumous publications include *The Burning Perch* (1936), containing some of his most intense work and *Collected Poems* (1966). *The Strings are False*, his unfinished autobiography, was published in 1965. He was made a CBE in 1958.

MacNeice was not as political as the rest of the 'Auden' group. His poetry has more of a balance with the personal and his range and variety is considerable, from the moving lyric of *Prayer Before Birth* to the comic *Bagpipe Music*. Alan Bennett, in *Poetry in Motion,* mentions MacNeice's lonely childhood that 'seems to have bred in him a melancholy and an aloofness that always set him apart' and attributes the underlying pessimism of much of his verse to this factor. He is perhaps the least known of the poets of his generation. Alan Bennett again sees elements in his private life that account for this: 'He had that very English fault; an overdose of irony. Irony stops you being whole-hearted, stops you from going overboard. But, of course, if you don't go overboard, you tend not to make a splash' (*Poetry in Motion).* MacNeice was a private man, 'riveted by doubt', therefore not as single-minded and positive as his more radical associates. Yet his sympathetic qualities have caused his poetry to endure and he is now recognised by some as, after Auden, the most important poet of the 1930s.

CHRISTOPHER MARLOWE (1564-93)

British playwright and poet

Born in Canterbury, the son of a shoemaker, he was educated at King's School, Canterbury and Corpus Christi College, Cambridge. The dissolute nature of his character showed itself early. As a young man he was arrested on charges of atheism and immorality. It is thought he began espionage work while still a student.

Like many 'University Wits', he was attracted to the London stage and on graduating from Cambridge he joined the Lord Admiral's players to become a busy playwright. There is some doubt about the chronological order of his plays but his first big success was certainly *Tamburlaine the Great* (1587). This deals with the pride and ambition of a central tyrant and was extravagant both in the language and action. The play's rhetoric, its 'high astounding terms', were delivered by Edward Alleyn, the company's leading actor. The sequel *The Second Part of Tamburlaine the Great* (1588) is somewhat inferior. Marlowe contrived to write of bold, defiant heroes whom we both admire and condemn.

The Jew of Malta, probably written around 1589 though not published until 1633, has a villain hero, Barabas. He, like Tamburlaine, has the best lines. The play is violent and grotesque and criticises contemporary religious values. It is thought the latter, inferior part of the play is by another hand.

Marlowe is most famous for his play *The Tragical History of Dr. Faustus* written 1588-9 and published in 1604. This, a precursor to Goethe's *Faust*, tells of a scholar who sells his soul to the devil in return for twenty-five years of earthly power. It contains some fine speeches and is important for its use of soliloquy, for character analysis and development. *Edward II* (c.1594) is more dramatic, with a better-woven plot and more development of historical character than had been seen before in historical plays. It may have influenced

Shakespeare's *Richard II* and paved the way for his more mature history plays.

Marlowe wrote two lesser plays, *Dido, Queen of Carthage* (1594 or earlier) and *The Massacre at Paris* (c.1589). He also translated Lucan's *Pharsalia* and Ovid's *Elegies*. The classics inspired him to write the erotic narrative poem, *Hero and Leander* (1598). This poem and the lyric, *Come Live with Me and Be My Love* from *The Passionate Shepherd* contain some of his finest poetry.

Marlowe's writing career lasted just six years, during which he wrote four major plays. His life was cut short before the age of thirty when he was killed in a tavern brawl. Mystery surrounds his death. Some believe he was assassinated because of his espionage activities or his blasphemous and outrageous behaviour. He was under warrant to appear before the Privy Council at the time. Marlowe set an example and influenced other writers in two main areas: he developed characterisation in order to heighten tragedy; he took the blank verse form, refined it and expanded its possibilities. His verse has a burning energy, variety of pace, splendid diction, sensuous richness and is full of imagery drawn from many sources. Its resonance and power led Ben Jonson to coin the phrase 'Marlowe's mighty line'. Marlowe freed Elizabethan literature, particularly its drama, from its formal constraints and paved the way for Shakespeare. Shakespeare acknowledged his influence and paid him a fine tribute in *As You Like It:*

'Dead Shepherd, now I find thy saw of might:
Who ever lov'd that lov'd not at first sight?'

ANDREW MARVELL (1621-1678)

British Metaphysical poet and satirist

Born in Winstead-in-Holderness, Yorkshire, the son of a Yorkshire clergyman who moved with his family to Hull in

1624. He attended Hull Grammar School and at twelve entered Trinity College, Cambridge, obtaining his degree in 1639. The classical reading he experienced there would prove to be a great influence on his poetry later.

Between 1643-47 he travelled throughout Europe, broadening his interests and studying languages. Shortly after his return, he was appointed tutor to Lord Fairfax's twelve year-old daughter at Nun Appleton House, Yorkshire. It was during this period (1650-52), with deep affection for his country surroundings, that he wrote most of his best lyrical verse. Poems such as *The Garden* and *Upon Appleton House* would later establish him as the greatest poet of this genre in the seventeenth century.

In 1653 he was again appointed tutor, this time to Cromwell's ward, William Dutton, and moved to Eton. *The First Anniversary* (1655) was the first of several eulogies on Cromwell and the Commonwealth. *An Horatian Ode upon Cromwell's Return from Ireland* is one of the greatest political poems in the English language. Marvell was an able linguist and was first appointed to assist Milton, now blind, and later, in 1657, to take over from him as Latin Secretary to the Council of State. It was Marvell who protected Milton from the Royalists after the Restoration and secured his release from prison.

Marvell entered Parliament, becoming MP for Hull in 1659, a post he held until his death. He enjoyed several trips abroad, travelling to Holland (1662-3) and - as secretary to the Earl of Carlisle - to Russia, Sweden and Denmark. He died in 1678, a much respected public figure.

By the time of his death, Marvell had acquired literary fame but it was his satirical writings that had made him popular. Although these satires were not officially published until 1689, copies were circulated and much enjoyed by the wits of the day. He wrote about politics, religion and affairs of state. Among the most popular at the time are *Clarendon's House Warming, The Loyal Scot* and *The Statue in Stocks-Market.* Even the subjects of his satires found them amusing. Marvell also wrote several verses against the inefficiency of the government of the King and his ministers - but Charles II is said to have been highly amused by *The Last Instructions to a Painter* (written in 1667 but published in 1689), attacking corruption at court. His powerful prose satire, *The Rehearsal Transpros'd* (published in two parts 1672-73), advocating tolerance for dissenters, was full of charm and humour. According to one contemporary, Gilbert Burnet, these were 'the wittiest books that have appeared in this age'.

In 1681, *Miscellaneous Poems* was published, very little of Marvell's verse having appeared before that date. His housekeeper, Mary Palmer, had submitted various papers found in his rooms to the printer. She claimed to be his widow and signed the preface, 'Mary Marvell'. Marvell's poetry, though not fully appreciated by his own generation, represents the best of metaphysical verse. It contains the subtlety of wit, the passionate argument and learned imagery of the metaphysicals (he particularly admired John Donne), combined with the clarity and control of the classical followers of Jonson and the grace of such Cavalier poets as Robert Herrick. His famous, seductive love poem, *To His Coy Mistress*, illustrates clearly the blend of passionate, eloquent and elaborate 'conceits' or images, handled with Marvell's distinctive control.

His poetry became more appreciated by nineteenth century critics, firstly by Charles Lamb, than those of his own age. Tennyson admired him as the 'green poet', the writer of the vivid pastoral poetry of the Nun Appleton days, the period before 1653, which includes *The Garden, The Picture of Little T.C. in a Prospect of Flowers* and *The Nymph Complaining for the Death of Her Fawn.* It was with the publication of Grierson's *Metaphysical Lyrics* and T.S. Eliot's book, *Andrew Marvell,* that his reputation grew in the twentieth century.

CARSON McCULLERS (1917-67)

American novelist, short story writer and dramatist

Born in Columbus, Georgia, the daughter of a well-to-do watchmaker and jeweller. She was considered a promising music student and was to attend the Juilliard School, but lost the tuition fees. She turned to creative writing instead, eventually gaining a place at Columbia University.

In 1936 she published *Wunderkind* in *Story* magazine, an autobiographical piece which deals with the theme of adolescent insecurity - a theme which would recur in her later fiction. Her first novel, *The Heart is a Lonely Hunter* (1940, filmed 1968), met with great acclaim. Despite some bizarre features (termed 'Southern Gothic') she showed psychological insight and compassion in depicting the loneliness and emotional rejection of her central character. It was considered to be a symbolic commentary on fascism and this made the book even more popular.

The spiritual isolation of the individual and their 'discovery' of themselves in love were common themes throughout her fiction. Her second novel, *Reflections in a Golden Eye* (1941, filmed in 1967 by John Huston with Marlon Brando and Elizabeth Taylor), again has 'gothic' elements, being a morbid tale of murder, infidelity and homosexual love. She was one of the first writers to deal with the latter. *The Ballad of Sad Café* followed in 1951, a collection of short stories dealing with love and isolation, originally published in serial form in *Harpers Bazaar* (1943). The title story was dramatised by Edward Albee in 1963 and a film version was made in 1990 directed by Simon Callow and starring Vanessa Redgrave.

Her next novel, wittier in style, is considered her best. *The Member of the Wedding* was published in 1946 and dramatised by McCullers herself. A success on Broadway, it won the

New York Drama Circle Award and two Donaldson Awards. It was filmed in 1952.

Other works include another play, *The Square Root of Wonderful* (1958), a novel *Clock Without Hands* (1961) dealing with racial problems and *The Mortgaged Heart* (1971), a collection of early stories. McCullers had always suffered from ill health. She suffered a series of strokes which finally killed her in 1967.

Her stories are set in the American South, where she lived for most of her life. They deal with those living in what she called, 'spiritual isolation' - the loners, the misfits, the outcasts, often physical freaks as well as emotional cripples. The mood of her books is also often melancholy, sometimes sentimental. She is said to have regarded herself as being vaguely freakish, like the grotesques that populated her fiction. Her private life contained plenty of the kind of traumas on which a writer with a preoccupation with psychological disturbance could draw. Apart from her frequent illnesses, she re-married a husband who, wounded from the war, turned to alcoholism, drug addiction and in 1953 committed suicide. She is considered one of the American South's leading writers.

JOHN MILTON (1608-74)

British poet

Born in Cheapside, London and educated at St. Paul's School and Christ's College, Cambridge - where he was known as 'the Lady of Christ's' for his puritan idealism. On graduating, he moved back home to the country in Horton, Buckinghamshire to study.

From 1637-39 he travelled abroad, chiefly in Italy, meeting many scholars and artists. On his return he published a series of controversial political pamphlets. In 1649 he was appointed Latin Secretary to the Commonwealth Council of State and retained this post until the Restoration, in spite of his blindness. When the monarchy was restored in 1660 he escaped the severe punishment inflicted on many prominent Parliamentary supporters. He retired to Buckinghamshire to write his greatest poetry. He died in London, where he is buried.

His work can be divided into three periods. He wrote his shorter poems during his time at university and while at Horton (1629-40). There followed a period of mainly prose writing (1640-60). His three greatest poems were written during the last years (1660-74). Between the two periods of writing poetry, Milton composed a number of sonnets. Some of these are among the finest ever written, particularly *On his Blindness* and *On the Late Massacre in Piedmont*. They show a command of the Italian form.

While still an undergraduate, Milton began to compose poems of remarkable maturity and promise. They include *Ode on the Morning of Christ's Nativity* (1629) and the poems, *On Shakespeare* (1630) and *On Arriving at the Age of Twenty-Three* (1631). These show an impressive command of language on both sacred and secular themes. His studies at Horton were extensive, taking in classics, languages, poetry, mathematics and music. His scholarship is evident in *L'Allegro* (dealing with the experiences of the happy man) and *Il Penseroso* (those of the thoughtful man) both written in the early 1630s. *Comus* (1634) is a masque and *Arcades* (1633) part of one. *Lycidas* (1637), in pastoral form, was written as an elegy for Edward King, a fellow student at Cambridge who drowned. The real subject of the poem is fear of premature death and unfulfilled ambition. These fears were Milton's own and give the poem its passionate sincerity.

His prose works, written when he was busy with public affairs, largely consist of pamphlets. They have a direct bearing on either his personal business (such as the two strong pamphlets on divorce written as a result of his own unsuccessful marriage) or public interest. The best of the latter is *Areopagitica* (1644), a speech for the Liberty of

Unlicensed Printing - a noble and impassioned plea for the freedom of the press. During the English Civil War he wrote a number of pamphlets supporting Cromwell and the Parliamentary cause and was rewarded by being made a minister of the Government. His eyesight had started to fail and by 1651 he was completely blind.

In *Paradise Lost* (1667), his masterpiece, Milton finally produced the great Christian epic he always hoped to write. At first it was divided into ten books but later edited into twelve. In form it follows the strict unity of the classical epic. In theme it deals with the fall of man, but by means of introduced narratives it covers the rebellion of Lucifer in heaven, celestial warfare and the expulsion of the rebel angels. The conception of the poem is vast and in it Milton draws upon Biblical, Classical, Medieval and Renaissance sources, using pagan imagery to serve a Christian purpose. The characters, especially Lucifer, are drawn on a gigantic scale. The type of blank verse used to express his great thoughts in this epic piece has great power and beauty, particularly when read aloud. It founded a tradition and was later much imitated. 'One of the greatest, most noble and sublime poems which either this age or nation has produced', wrote Dryden. *Paradise Regained* (1671), telling of Christ's temptation and victory, complements the earlier poem but lacks its rich use of imagination and ornate themes. There is little action and the characters are less interesting, though there are a few outstanding passages.

Samson Agonistes (1671) is a tragedy in the Greek style. Written predominantly in blank verse, it contains passages of great metrical freedom and originality and some rhyme. It describes the last days of Samson when he is blind and a prisoner. Some lines reflect Milton's own feelings, having been blind for about twenty years when the poem was written.

Several features are common throughout Milton's poetry. All through his life his religious fervour was unshakeable. He himself said his chief motive in *Paradise Lost* was to 'justify the ways of God to men'. This religious tendency is apparent in the choice of religious subjects, the sense of responsibility and moral exaltation, the fondness for preaching (a weakness in *Paradise Lost*) and the narrow puritanical outlook. Secondly, there is a strong classical influence, the pagan and sensuous interwoven with the religious severity. Milton's learning was wide and he wrote Latin prose and verse as freely as English. The classical influence is apparent in the choice of classical or semi-classical forms - the epic, the Greek tragedy, the pastoral and the sonnet, the elaborate descriptions and use of simile in *Paradise Lost*, the fondness for classical illusion, the dignity and precision of style.

As a poet Milton was not so much an innovator as a refiner of style. His own strict discipline gave grace and dignity to each verse form he adopted and his use of metre singled him out among his contemporaries.

In literature Milton occupies an important central or transitional position between the Elizabethans and the 'Age of Reason'.

BEN OKRI (born 1959)

Nigerian novelist and short story writer

Born in Lagos. Soon afterwards, he went to London with his father, who was studying law, and spent his earliest years in Peckham. He returned to Nigeria when he was seven but because of the family's financial difficulties was withdrawn several times from school. As a result he educated himself at home while writing articles and stories.

He attended Urhobo College, Wani and won a place at the University of Essex to study comparative literature but, unable to support himself financially, left without taking a degree. Again he moved to London, often sleeping rough. He first came to prominence with two semi-autobiographical novels, *Flowers and Shadows* (1980), which he wrote when he was nineteen, and *The Landscape Within* (1981). Okri was clearly a young writer with promise. What distinguished him from previous African writers was his examination of personal feelings rather than the historical or political issues of his country.

During the 1980s he was poetry editor of *West Africa* magazine and worked for the BBC World Service (1984-5), which supplemented his income. Two collections of short stories followed: *Incidents at the Shrine* (1986) and *Stars of the New Curfew* (1989). These paint a realistic picture of village and urban life during the Nigerian Civil War. Although he won literary prizes, it was not until he won the Booker Prize in 1991 with his novel, *The Famished Road,* that he reached a real audience. Narrated by Azaro, a 'spirit child', it mixes elements of the supernatural with the vivid, often harsh, reality of life in a shanty town. Some of the dream-like qualities he explores are also present in the short stories.

His first volume of poetry, *An African Elegy,* was published in 1992. *Songs of Enchantment,* a sequel to *The Famished Road,* appeared in 1993. Ben Okri has established himself as one of the leading young writers of the time.

WILFRID OWEN (1893-1918)

British poet, one of the group known as the War Poets

Born at Oswestry in Shropshire, where his father was a station master, educated at Birkenhead Institute and University of London. In 1913 he worked as a private tutor near Bordeaux and during this time is reputed to have been influenced by modern French poetry.

Despite poor health, he enlisted in the Artist's Rifles in 1915, and was later commissioned in the Manchester Regiment. He served in the trenches in France from January 1917 to June 1917 when, suffering from concussion and trench fever on the Somme, he was invalided to hospital in Edinburgh. Here he met Siegfried Sassoon, who offered advice and encouraged him in his writing. Soon afterwards, Sassoon introduced Owen to Robert Graves and Robert Nichols and the four poets stayed together on leave in North Wales.

Owen returned to the same battalion at the Front as Company Commander. In October he was awarded the Military Cross for exceptional bravery in the field. He was killed by machine gun fire on November 4th 1918, a week before the Armistice was declared, while endeavouring to get his company across the Sambre Canal.

Only five of Owen's poems were published during his lifetime and they made little impression. *Poems*, with an Introduction by Siegfried Sassoon (1920) and *Collected Poems*, with an Introduction by Edmund Blunden (1931) established his reputation as the outstanding poet of World War I. The poems were collected again in 1963, edited by Cecil Day-Lewis. *Collected Letters* was published in 1967 and a biography by Jon Stallworthy in 1974.

Owen's poems have been used by composer Benjamin Britten in one of his major compositions, *War Requiem*. John Wain has written: 'Is there a finer war poem in world literature than *Anthem for Doomed Youth*?' And Sir Osbert Sitwell wrote of *Strange Meeting*: 'as great a poem as exists in our tongue'.

MERVYN PEAKE (1911-1968)

British novelist, artist, poet

Born in China, the son of a missionary doctor, educated in Tientsin and, on returning to England in 1923, at Eltham College, Kent. He trained as an artist at the Royal Academy Schools. He spent three years with an artists' colony on the island of Sark, returning to London to teach at the Westminster School of Art (1935-39). It was here he met his wife, Maeve Gilmore, a student, who became a successful painter. They had three children. His first book was written during this period - a fantastical pirate story for children, *Captain Slaughterboard Drops Anchor* (1939), which he illustrated himself.

In 1943 he was invalided out of the army because of a nervous breakdown but toward the end of the War was commissioned as official War artist. A visit to Belsen concentration camp in 1945 greatly affected him. He returned to teaching after the War and again to Sark, the setting for his allegorical novel, *Mr Pye* (1953). Ill health forced him to retire in 1960 and he died tragically early of Parkinson's Disease.

Peake was an outstanding illustrator not only of his own work but also of Lewis Carroll's *Alice in Wonderland* and *The Hunting of the Snark*, R.L. Stevenson's *Treasure Island*, *Grimm's Household Tales* and Coleridge's *The Rime of the Ancient Mariner*. He greatly admired the work of Edgar Allan Poe and Franz Kafka. His own illustrations and writing explore similar dark recesses of the imagination. He drew the grotesque, haunted, distorted figures of the characters in the *Gormenghast* novels before writing about them.

In the *Gormenghast* trilogy Peake created one of the greatest fantasy worlds in modern fiction. The three books are *Titus Groan* (1946), *Gormenghast* (1950) and *Titus Alone* (1959), which was influenced by his visit to Belsen. It is a Gothic epic, set in the surreal, sometimes nightmarish world of Titus, 77th Earl of Groan and the crumbling castle of Gormenghast. Full of colourful characters and rich language, the sequence attracted a mixed reception initially but later developed a cult following - particularly after J.R.R. Tolkien started a vogue for supernatural fantasy adventure with the publication of his *Lord of the Rings* in the mid 1950s. Peake's three books were re-issued as a trilogy in 1967.

Peake also wrote poetry for both children and adults - long narratives, lyrical love poems and nonsense verse. *The Glassblowers* (1950), together with his novel *Gormenghast*, earned him the W.H. Heinemann Foundation Prize in 1950. *Rhymes Without Reason* (1944) and *The Rhyme of the Flying Bomb* (1962), a ballad of the Blitz, are other notable works. *A Book of Nonsense* was published posthumously in 1972.

Peake wrote four plays, one of which was performed (*The Wit to Woo*) and also designed sets and costumes for the theatre. He adapted his work for the radio and wrote short stories for several periodicals. His widow, Maeve Gilmore, has written her own memoir, *A World Away* (1970).

SYLVIA PLATH (1932-63)

American poet and novelist

Born in Boston, America, the daughter of a professor at Boston University. His death in 1940 contributed to the periods of depression which recurred throughout her life, culminating in her suicide in London at a tragically early age.

She came to England on a Fulbright scholarship and, while at Newnham College, Cambridge, met the British poet Ted Hughes (qv). They married in 1956 and for a time she returned to her old college, Smith in Massachusetts, to teach. She attended lectures given by the American poet Robert Lowell at Boston University. He became a great influence.

In 1959, Plath and Hughes left America to settle permanently in Britain, living at first in London before moving to Devon in 1961. They had two children. She had early literary success, winning a fiction contest while still at college. Only two books were published in her lifetime: a volume of verse, *The Colossus* (1960), and a semi-autobiographical novel, *The Bell Jar* (1963) under the pen name Victoria Lucas. The title refers to the central image: the way in which a person suffering from mental illness is separated from the world, as if encased in a glass dome.

It was the second volume of poems, *Ariel* (1965), published after her suicide, which established her reputation. These poems, showing a courageous and controlled treatment of themes which deal with extreme and painful states of mind, aroused a great deal of interest on publication. They combine bold imagery with original but controlled rhythms, their style almost unique in the English language. Similar images recur almost like an obsession: for instance, the shore-bound spectator looking out at a beckoning sea. Much of the symbolism in these poems is personal, describing the house in Devon and its surroundings. She used many of her own experiences - *Lady Lazarus* is based on her two previous suicide attempts; *Daddy* on the early loss of her father; *Tulips* on a week spent in hospital. These personal references have led to comparisons with the 'confessional' poetry of Robert Lowell - but her poetry has an extreme and painful quality that makes it entirely original. In many ways she is more of an English than an American writer, her husband Ted Hughes having an important influence on her work.

M.L. Rosenthal in *The New Poets* suggests these poems are 'written out of a strange kind of terror, the calm centre of hysteria'. She makes a similar comment herself. In a recording for the British Council she declared 'one should be able to control and manipulate experiences, even the most terrifying …. with an informed and intelligent mind'. The remaining months of her life, by this time separated from her husband, were a period of intense creativity. Writing in a state of extreme, almost neurotic, excitement about obsessive and emotional states of mind, she sometimes produced three to four poems a day, describing them as 'long and thin like myself'. The pressure under which she wrote prompted A. Alvarez to remark, 'Poetry of this order is a murderous art'. It was the unfavourable reception given to *The Bell Jar* that led to her suicide (she gassed herself) within a month of its publication.

Since her death, her name and work has taken on the quality of a legend and even that of cult status in some circles. Looking beyond the sensationalism of her life and death, the distinguishing qualities of her writing are its personal intensity, sharp imagery and unique rhythms. The enduring power of her work is to fascinate, to inspire and to challenge the way we think about woman's identity.

Other posthumous publications include *Crossing the Water* (1971), *Winter Trees* (1971), *Letter Home: Correspondence 1950-63* (1975), *Johnny Panic and the Bible of Dreams* (collected prose pieces 1977). *Collected Poems* (1981), edited by Ted Hughes, won the Pulitzer Prize. *The Journals of Sylvia Plath* were published in 1983.

EDGAR ALLAN POE (1809-49)

American poet and fiction writer

The son of a family of actors, Poe was born in Boston. He became an orphan in early childhood, and was brought up by John Allan, a tobacco exporter from Richmond, Virginia. Though he was never formally adopted, Edgar Poe inserted his guardian's name into his own in 1824 and used it for the rest of his life.

He was educated at Stoke Newington in England and went on to the University of Virginia for a year. In 1827 he paid for the anonymous publication of *Tamerlane and other Poems.* A year later he enlisted in the U.S. Army. Allan, from whom he had become estranged, procured his discharge and Poe entered West Point, but was dismissed in 1831. Poe then turned to journalism, living with a relative in Baltimore, whose thirteen year old daughter, his cousin Virginia, he married in 1836. He became editor of various periodicals, including the *Southern Literary Messenger* in which he published some of his best stories. He died in Baltimore from a combination of alcoholic poisoning, heart failure and epilepsy.

Tales of the Grotesque and Arabesque appeared in 1839; *The Murders in the Rue Morgue* in 1841; *The Gold Bug* in 1843; *The Raven*, the first poem which won him wide popularity, in 1845. Other verse includes: *To Helen, Israfeil, The City in the Sea, The Haunted Palace* and *Dreamland* between 1831 and 1844. *Ulalume* appeared in 1847, *For Annie, Annabel Lee* and *The Bells* in 1849. Famous tales include *The Fall of the House of Usher* (1839), *A Descent into the Maelstrom* (1841), *The Masque of the Red Death* and *The Mystery of Marie Roget* (1842), *The Purloined Letter* (1845), *The Cask of Amontillado* and *The Facts in the Case of M. Waldemar* (1846). Poe also wrote much literary criticism.

He was much admired by Baudelaire and Dostoevsky and in Britain by Swinburne, Wilde, Rossetti and Yeats. Indeed, Yeats considered Poe to be 'always and for all lands a great lyric poet'.

SAMUEL RICHARDSON (1689-1761)

British novelist

Born near Derby, the son of a furniture maker, he spent his childhood in London. He received little formal education but entertained his school fellows with stories. By the age of thirteen he was writing letters for young lovers. His father could not afford the classical education needed for the clergy and in 1706 apprenticed him to a printer. In this profession Richardson prospered. He married his former master's daughter in 1721 and set up on his own. He combined printing and publishing, as most printers did at the time, and in 1723 began issuing *The True Briton*, a Tory journal.

His professional life was thriving but tragedy struck his personal life. By the early 1730s all six of his children and his wife had died. He remarried in 1733, the daughter of another printer, and published *The Apprentice's Vade Mecum*, a guide to moral behaviour. In 1739 his own moral version of *Aesop's Fables* was published.

In 1738 he bought a house in Fulham that was to become a place for him to meet and give readings to his growing circle of friends and authors. His first novel, *Pamela; or Virtue Rewarded,* was published anonymously in 1740. It had taken two months to write and had begun as a series of 'familiar letters'. Richardson was inspired to combine them into a form of narrative and he subsequently used the epistolary form for all of his novels. It became a great success in Britain and abroad and for its moral tone was recommended to be read from pulpits. *Pamela* had its critics, among them Henry

Fielding who replied with his own version, *Shamela,* attacking the dubious moral tone of the original.

Richardson's business prospered and in 1742 he won a lucrative contract to print Parliamentary Journals. He was popular as a novelist and his circle of friends increased to include many admiring young ladies, his 'honorary daughters', whom he frequently consulted for their comments when writing his next novel, *Clarissa. Clarissa Harlowe* (1747-8), published in three instalments, is considered his best novel, despite being one of the longest novels in the English language. It was also well received in Europe, being translated into French, Dutch and German. There were complaints about its length and 'indecency'. Because of this, it proved less popular in England than *Pamela.*

His next project was not to have a heroine but to be about a high minded English gentleman. He had become friends with Dr. Johnson and asked him in 1752 to read the draft manuscript of what was to become *The History of Sir Charles Grandison,* which appeared in seven volumes in 1753-54. He had never forgiven Fielding's attack on *Pamela* and it was thought that this portrait of male virtue was a counter-attack for the immoral tendencies of *Tom Jones.* Again there were doubts about the novel's morality and length. Taking up a suggestion from Dr. Johnson, he published, in 1755, a volume of selections from the three novels, that he thought contained his best work (*A Collection of the Moral and Instructive Sentiments ... in the Histories of Pamela, Clarissa and Sir Charles Grandison*). When Johnson's famous Dictionary was published in 1755 there were more references to *Clarissa* than any other work of fiction.

Richardson continued to revise his novels and was active in his business until he died. In 1754-5 he was elected Master of the Stationers Company. In 1756 he was asked by Blackwell for his advice on the reform of the Oxford University Press and in 1760 purchased a share of the patent of the printer to the King.

It is generally agreed that Samuel Richardson was the main founder of the English novel and *Pamela* the first 'modern' novel that dealt with moral questions in a social context, avoiding 'the improbable and the marvellous' of previous authors. What he did extraordinarily well was to examine the human heart and the psychological make-up of his characters by presenting their thoughts and feelings. The epistolary style helped this enormously, as well as adding immediacy. He was particularly praised for his insight into female characters. In *Clarissa*, he also created Lovelace, a masterly villain-hero - a complex man whose villainy is only gradually revealed. The characterisation of Lovelace helped inspire Choderlos de Laclos's Valmont in *Les Liaisons Dangereuses* (1782).

'Richardson was well qualified to be the discoverer of a new style of writing, for he was a cautious, deep and minute examiner of the human heart'

Sir Walter Scott

On the length of his novels Dr. Johnson wrote...

'if you were to read Richardson for the story, your impatience would be so much fretted that you would hang yourself ...' He also believed, 'There is more knowledge of the human heart in one letter of Richardson's than in all of *Tom Jones*'

Dr. Johnson

On moral intention, Samuel Richardson in *Preface to Clarissa* (1747-8):

'I thought the story, if written in an early and natural manner, suitable to the simplicity of it, might possibly introduce a new species of writing that might possibly turn young people into a course of reading different from the pomp and parade of romance writing, and dismissing the improbable and marvellous, with which novels generally abound, might tend to promote the cause of religion and virtue.'

ELIZABETH RIDDELL (born 1910)

New Zealand poet and journalist

Born and educated in Napier, New Zealand. Shortly after leaving school she moved to Australia to embark on a career in journalism. In 1930 she worked for *Smith's Weekly* of Sydney and the Sydney *Sunday Sun.* She married the journalist E.N. Greatorex in 1935 and during the Second World War worked as a war correspondent, returning to Australia in 1945.

Since then she has become a respected journalist, freelance book reviewer and feature writer. Altogether she has published four collections of poetry, the two most recent being *From the Midnight Courtyard* (1989) and *Selected Poems* (1992).

Elizabeth Riddell has been a journalist all her life - 'I always meant to be a poet, never a journalist, but life plays these tricks' - and has worked in the U.K. and United States as well as Australia. She has said that her career as a journalist has influenced both the style and the content of her poetry. Her work has been commended for its accessibility, conciseness and the way in which she uses ordinary subjects to evoke an emotional response. Her descriptions are often luxuriant and show an 'unjournalistic' aestheticism. Her early work tends to rhyme, her later poetry is less formal. She has been awarded the Grace Level Prize as well as the Walkley award.

PAUL SCOTT (1920-78)

British novelist

Born in North London, the son of a commercial artist. Educated at Winchmore Hill Collegiate School. He later served in the army during World War II in India, Burma and Malaya. He was fascinated by those countries, which he made the setting for most of his novels. He lived mainly in London, working at first in publishing (reviewing books for *The Times, The Guardian, The Daily Telegraph* and *Country Life*) and later spending ten years as a literary agent. In 1960 he left the agency to become a full-time writer.

He was elected Fellow of the Royal Society of Literature in 1963 and in his later years he divided his time between his London home and the University of Tulsa, Oklahoma where he was a visiting lecturer.

Many of his earlier novels deal with Anglo-Indian relationships. His second novel, *Johnnie Sahib* (1952), won him a literary fellowship and his reputation was made the following year with *Alien Sky* (1953). This was adapted for radio and television. Much of what followed did not meet with great success, the best work being *The Bird of Paradise* (1962), which examines the effects brought about by changes in history. This preoccupation is seen again in *The Corrida at San Felio* (1964), in which he explores several different viewpoints and makes use of a fragmented narrative structure.

This method is seen throughout his main achievement, *The Raj Quartet* (1976). This consists of four inter-connected novels - *The Jewel in the Crown* (1966), *The Day of the Scorpion* (1968), *The Towers of Silence* (1971 - winner of the Yorkshire Post fiction award) and *A Division of the Spoils* (1975). On a vast scale and with a huge cast of characters, Scott sets the Quartet in India during the final five years of British Rule (1942-7). The racial, religious and personal conflicts are highlighted by the change towards Independence. Popular success came not so much with the quartet but with its coda, *Staying On* (1977), dealing in a gentler, more satirical way with the lives of two of the characters after Independence. This won him the Booker Prize and enhanced his reputation. *Staying On* was adapted for television in 1981 and *The Raj Quartet* as *The Jewel in the Crown* was screened in 1984, having taken four years to adapt. This acclaimed series gained Scott a wider readership and more popularity than in his lifetime.

Despite his novels, Paul Scott did not have a particular affinity with India, nor a romanticised view of Imperialism. According to Roland Grant (editor and first publisher of *The Raj Quartet*), it was 'the inter-play, emotional and political, between the nations [that] fascinated him as did the relationship between individuals'. In his exploration of such relationships against the vividly depicted background of India, Scott is reminiscent of Forster. It is the unique way in which Scott chose to structure his narrative that marks *The Raj Quartet* as a literary landmark. The *New York Times* called it:

> 'a major work, a glittering combination of brilliant craftsmanship, psychological perception and objective reporting ... Rarely have the sounds and smells and total atmosphere been so evocatively suggested.'

PERCY BYSSHE SHELLEY (1792-1822)

British poet

Born near Horsham, Sussex to a wealthy family: his father was an MP. Shelley had a brilliant mind but his wayward behaviour revealed itself from the beginning. He attended Eton and was mocked by the other boys for his eccentric ways, earning the nickname 'Mad Shelley'. He was reprimanded by his tutors for his dangerous chemical and occult experiments. He also started writing poetry with his sister while still at school and had two Gothic novels published privately.

He subsequently went to Oxford where he became a political radical, dressing eccentrically, and advocating vegetarianism, free love and atheism. He co-wrote *The Necessity of Atheism* and as a result of the ensuing scandal was sent down from Oxford. His elopement and subsequent marriage that same year, 1811, to the sixteen year old Harriet Westwood caused a break with the family and a renouncement of his inheritance.

For the next three years the Shelleys lived a nomadic existence, spending time in Scotland, Wales and Dublin. Here he wrote pamphlets against English rule. In 1813, *Queen Mab* was published but to no great acclaim. He left his pregnant wife for Mary Wollstonecraft Godwin. In 1814 he left England with Mary and her fifteen year old stepsister, Claire Clairmont. Clairmont was to live with them, on and off, for years. Their combined journals of this trip were revised by Mary Shelley and published as *History of a Six Weeks Tour* (1817).

On returning to England, Shelley experienced financial difficulties and, while staying near Windsor, wrote *Alastor* (1815), his first important long poem, a kind of spiritual autobiography. When Harriet committed suicide in 1816, Shelley immediately married Mary and, together with Claire, moved to Switzerland. This move was instigated by Claire who hoped to resume her affair with Lord Byron. Despite their differences, Byron and Shelley formed an important friendship that summer on the shores of Lake Geneva. Shelley was inspired to write his first truly great poem, *Hymn to Intellectual Beauty*. He also wrote another philosophical poem, *Mont Blanc*, and Mary Shelley started writing *Frankenstein*. Shelley returned to England where Leigh Hunt introduced him to Keats and Hazlitt.

In 1817 *An Address to the People on the Death of Princess Charlotte*, his finest political pamphlet, was published and he worked on *The Revolt of Islam* (1818). After a year in England, discouraged by the political atmosphere and in poor health, the Shelleys, their children and Claire Clairmont left England for the last time for Italy in 1818. He wrote, 'I am regarded as a rare prodigy of crime and pollution, whose look might even infect'. His renewed acquaintance with Byron inspired *Julian and Maddalo*.

His last few years in Italy were to be his most creative period. *The Mask of Anarchy* (a political protest poem inspired by the Peterloo massacre), *Peter Bell the Third* (a satirical joke on Wordsworth), *The Cenci* (a verse tragedy) and his other great lyrical drama, *Prometheus Unbound* (a visionary idea for the reform of mankind), were written in 1819-20. During this 'Pisan' period (1820-1), enamoured of Italy, he wrote some of his finest lyrics - *Ode to the West Wind, To a Skylark, The Cloud* - and shorter poems such as *To the Moon, The Two Spirits* and *The Aziola.* Byron had moved in with the Shelleys in 1821 and the group formed the centre of a circle of ex-patriots. As well as lyrics, Shelley wrote political odes such as *The Liberty, To Naples* (1820), propaganda poems (*Song to the Men of England* and *Sonnet: England 1819*) and a verse drama, *Hellas* (1822), written to raise money for the Greek War of Independence. His essay, *A Defence of Poetry* (1821, published 1840), was written at this time, an exposition of the Romantic point of view that 'poets are the unacknowledged legislators of the world'.

Although much of his late verse was political, the news of Keats' death in 1821 prompted *Adonais*, a moving elegy and one of his best poems. After the break up of the Pisa group, the Shelleys moved to the village of Lerici on the Bay of Spezia. He began his last major poem, *The Triumph of Life* (published 1824). He also wrote a sequence of short lyrics for Jane Williams (*The Keen Stars are Twinkling, When the Lamp is Shattered* and the bleak *Lines Written in the Bay of Lerici*), who with her husband, Edward, had moved to Lerici. Shelley's relationship with Mary had become strained, all but one of his children had died and he was having bizarre hallucinations - almost certainly as a result of the laudanum he was taking for a nervous disorder. On the way back from a meeting with Leigh Hunt, Shelley and Edward Williams were drowned in the Bay of Spezia, Shelley's body identified by a copy of Keats' poems in his pocket. He was not quite thirty.

After his death, his family attempted to repair the tarnished image of their son, an 'ineffectual angel', by encouraging the publication of Mary Shelley's edition of *The Poetical Works* (1839). *Poetical Pieces* (1823) and *Posthumous Poems* (1824) also appeared. Shelley was the most radical of all the Romantics and there is a fusion between his life and his work - he spent nearly all his life in exile for putting into practice the romantic and political idealism that he wrote about in his pamphlets, essays and poems. He is remembered for his lyric poetry, among the best in the language. Other features of his work are a visionary, prophetic quality, tied up with the more radical tendencies of the Romantics towards social injustice. The shorter lyrics often deal with the spiritual aspects of nature - he peoples them with phantoms and airy beings. He is frequently concerned with thoughts of death and despair. His descriptions are imaginative and immediate, often making use of personification. As with all great lyric poets, his style is simple and flexible, with clarity of phrase and purity of language. His limitations tend to be in the longer poems where his rhapsodising becomes tedious and the symbolism sometimes confusing. The shorter poems, being more concentrated, are more effective.

In his lifetime his opinions obscured his powers as a poet ('that atheist Shelley', remarked Scott) but after his death his reputation rose and, despite the colourful nature of his lifestyle, he became a favourite poet of the Victorians.

LOUIS SIMPSON (born 1923)

American poet, playwright, novelist and critic

Born in Jamaica, he emigrated to the USA in 1940, attending the University of Columbia before serving in the US Army during World War II. He returned to Columbia to complete his PhD after the war and then went to teach at the Universities of California, Berkeley and the State University of New York at Stony Brook.

He has written a novel, two plays and works of criticism. He is, however, best known for his poetry, which combines a colloquial, often ironic, tone with subject matter that is often mythical and dream-like. His first volume of poems, *The Arrivistes*, appeared in 1949. Subsequent works include *Good News of Death* (1955), *Andromeda* (1956, a play), *A Dream of Governors* (1959) and *Riverside Drive* (1962), a novel about a young Jamaican man's experiences in New York and the Army.

At the End of the Open Road won him the Pulitzer Prize in 1963 (and includes the long poem, *The Marriage of Pocahontas*, fusing historical fact and myth). Other publications include *Adventures of the Letter l* (1971), *Searching for the Ox* (1976), *North of Jamaica* (1972, an autobiography), *Caviar at the Funeral* (1980), *People Live Here* (1983), *In the Room we Share* (1990), *Wei Wei and Other Friends* (1990), *The Best Hour of the Night* (1984), *Collected Poems* (1988) and *Selected Prose* (1989).

He has been responsible for critical works such as *James Hogg, A Critical Study* (1962), *Three on a Tower* (1975 - essays on Ezra Pound, T. S. Eliot and William Carlos Williams) and *A Revolution in Taste* (1978 - studies of Dylan Thomas, Allen Ginsberg, Sylvia Plath and Robert Lowell who 'created art out of the confusion of their lives'). *A Company of Poets* (1981) was published as part of a 'poets on poetry' series and he has jointly edited an influential anthology *The New Poets of England and America* (1957).

STEVIE SMITH (1902-71)

British poet and novelist

Born Florence Margaret Smith in Hull, she moved to her aunt's house in Palmer's Green, North London when she was three and lived there for the rest of her life. Her father had joined the merchant navy when she was a child and she saw very little of him. She was brought up by her mother and aunt, whom she adored - the 'lion aunt' who was to feature so often in her work. Her childhood was overshadowed by her own tuberculosis and her mother's unhappy marriage, illness and death (when Stevie was only sixteen).

She was educated at Palmer's Green High School and the North London Collegiate School for Girls. She adopted the name 'Stevie' when her riding was compared to that of the famous jockey, Steve Donaghue. On leaving school she went to Secretarial College and then into her first and only job as secretary with Newnes-Pearson, the magazine publishing house. Here she remained for thirty years. She wrote her first novel, which is the best known, on the firm's yellow copying paper, calling it *Novel on Yellow Paper* (1936). Like much of her poetry, it is both serious and comic. The two subsequent novels, *Over the Frontier* (1938) and *The Holiday* (1949, the one she preferred), are more melancholic. All three books are autobiographical.

Smith considered herself primarily a poet - she began writing fiction only when her early poems failed to find a publisher - and it is for her poetry that she is remembered. Altogether eight volumes of poetry were published. The first is the best known, *A Good Time was Had by All* (1937), which was accompanied by her own simplistic line drawings. These were to feature in much of her work.

During the 1950s she underwent a period of depression, partly because she had difficulty finding magazines to accept her poetry. This depression instigated the writing of the poem *Not Waving but Drowning* in the spring of 1953 and also brought about a nervous breakdown and suicide attempt the following year. Also in 1953, she left publishing to care for her aunt, who was now bedridden. Her career revived with *Selected Poems* (1962), which received excellent reviews (including one from Philip Larkin). Being included in the Penguin Modern Poets Series in the early 1960s also gave her greater recognition. Her widest popularity came in the 1960s when, well into middle age, she began a series of poetry readings of her own work, both live and recorded. The simple metres of her poems were suitable for reading aloud and her idiosyncratic delivery and eccentric but engaging personality endeared her to a wide audience, particularly amongst the young.

Other volumes include, *Mother what is a Man?* (1942), *Harold's Leap* (1950), *The Frog Prince and other Poems* (1966), *The Best Beast* (1969) and *Scorpion and other Poems* (1972). Posthumous publications include *Collected Poems* (1975), *Selected Poems* (1978) and *Me Again: Uncollected Writings of Stevie Smith* (1981). She received the Cholmondeley Award and in 1969 the Queen's Gold Medal for Poetry. She died of a brain tumour aged 68. Hugh Whitemore wrote a play, *Stevie*, based on her works which was later made into a film starring Glenda Jackson.

To consider the life of a writer can sometimes lead to a better understanding of their work. This is true of Stevie Smith. The very ordinary, somewhat restricted life she led produced poetry free from 'bookishness'. It is simple, almost childlike in its expression yet this naïve style is flexible and able to express a wide variety of sombre emotions - loneliness, sexual anxiety, conflict with faith, the obsession with death - that lie beneath the surface, as they did in her own life as a spinster in the North London suburbs. Anthony Thwaite called her 'primarily a poet of the odd, the disconcerting, the unexpected' and it is this anarchic quality, together with her barbed wit, that made the spirit of her poetry very much in tune with the late 1960s. It is her originality that marks her as an important poet for any generation.

'The very modernity of Stevie Smith's verse seemed to come from its old fashioned quality: it seemed that her doggerel style, and Edward Lear-like drawings, were a way of poking fun at the pretentiousness of all the traditional poets in the school anthologies'.

George Macbeth

STEPHEN SPENDER (1909-1995)

British poet and critic

Born in London, the son of a distinguished liberal journalist. Educated at University College School in London and University College, Oxford, where he met W.H. Auden, C. Day Lewis, Louis MacNeice and, through Auden, Christopher Isherwood. This group of young writers, together with Spender, made a great impact in the 1930s with their poetry and left-wing political enthusiasms.

As a young man, Spender travelled widely in Europe to Austria, Germany in the 1920s and to Spain during the Civil War where he was engaged as a propagandist for the Republicans. The rise of fascism and growing unemployment sharpened his political awareness. He briefly joined the Communist Party, contributed to *The Daily Worker* and wrote the verse play, *The Trial of a Judge* (1938), performed by The Group Theatre.

His first volume of poetry appeared in 1930: *Twenty Poems* followed by *Poems* (1933), a much publicised volume that had a great impact and is considered to contain his best work. The poems sum up the romantic and political yearnings of the period and, with this and subsequent volumes such as *The Still Centre* (1939) and *Ruins and Visions* (1942), Spender achieved a high profile in the 1930s. He also defended the use of political influence in poetry in *The Destructive Element* (1935).

Although primarily a poet, he had a keen interest in cultural and world affairs, and from 1939 to 1941 he co-edited *Horizon* (with Cyril Connolly) and later (1953-67) the magazine *Encounter*. He worked for the National Fire Service and the Foreign Office during the Second World War. He worked for UNESCO after the war and during the 1950s and 1960s held various visiting professorships in America. He became Professor of English Literature at University College, London (1970-77).

Spender did not publish so much poetry after the war. Volumes that did appear include *Poems of Dedication* (1947), *Edge of Being* (1949), *Collected Poems 1928-53* (1954), *Selected Poems* (1965) and *The Generous Days* (1969). His main output was critical articles. He contributed to *The God that Failed* (1949), revealing a move away from communism, and other main works include *The Creative Element* (1953), *The Struggle of the Modern* (1963) and *Love-Hate Relations: A Study in Anglo-American Sensibilities* (1974). He also devoted time to writing his autobiography, *World Within World* (1951).

As well as writing verse, critical works and political reflections, Spender has been a translator, mainly of German literature, and also of an important *Oedipus* trilogy. His first novel, *The Temple,* was published in 1988 and he collaborated with the painter David Hockney on *China Diary* (1982, after a journey they made together). He was writing well into old age: *Collected Poems 1928-83* was published in 1985, his *Journal 1939-83* in 1987 and *Dolphins* (1994) when he was 85. He was also active as a speaker at literary functions and, according to friend and fellow poet Alan Ross, 'until his dying day … would accept almost any invitation to read or perform, no matter how far afield or humble. He genuinely liked the feel of an audience, an opportunity to meet new people and engage in debate'.

He received many awards: the CBE in 1962, The Queen's Gold Medal for Poetry in 1971, a Knighthood in 1983 and the PEN Golden Pen Award for Services to Literature in 1995.

Stephen Spender has suffered somewhat from having such a high profile in the 1930s. It is these poems that tend to be the most anthologised. It was his poem, *The Pylons,* in *Poems* (1933) that gave the *Pylon Poets* their name. He also fell under Auden's shadow and in the later years was seen more as a surviving poet of that time than a modern writer. He was always interested in what was going on, not only in the world of literature but also in politics, art and music and he became a patriarchal figure of the establishment.

Alan Ross wrote on his death that he was 'an unusual mixture of the worldly and simple, his rather grand social life as a guest on the celebrity circuit alternating with periods of quiet (at home) ... He bathed in attention, but the attention was not spurious - it derived from a life devoted to writing, and one that took poetry away from the study and into the public domain'.

LISA ST AUBIN DE TERAN (born 1953)

British novelist

Born in London to an English mother and South American father. Educated at James Allen's Girls' School, which she left at sixteen to marry a Venezuelan landowner. She lived on their estate in the Andes for seven years, absorbing the stories told by family and servants. These would provide material for her first novel. She returned to England where she began her literary career by writing poetry. *The Streak* (1980) was published privately.

In 1982 she married the poet George Macbeth and lived for a time in Norfolk. Her mother's death, together with the break up of her second marriage, brought about a nervous breakdown which has influenced much of her later work.

Some of her novels draw on her experiences in South America particularly *Slow Train to Milan* (1984), *The Tiger* (1985) and *The High Place* (1985), the latter containing some poems about the estate workers. Other works include *Keepers of the House* (1982), a largely autobiographical story which won a Somerset Maugham Award; *Black Idol* (1987); and *Off the Rails, Memoirs of a Train Addict* (1989) which reviews her use of railways as a 'means of truancy' while at school. *The Marble Mountain* (1989) contains a collection of stories of death and surreal horrors and in *Joanna* (1980) she draws upon her own mother, grandmother and great-grandmother for a tale of three generations. She won the Eric Gregory Poetry Award in 1983. Her second volume of memoirs, *A Valley in Italy*, describes her life with third husband, painter Robbie Duff-Scott, and an extended family in a villa in Umbria.

PATRICK SÜSKIND (born 1949)

German novelist

Patrick Süskind originally studied history in Munich and was writing for television before his first novel, *Perfume,* was published in 1985. Described as a 'tour de force of obsession and disgust', it made a great impact and brought the author international recognition. A second novel *The Pigeon* (1987) is similar in theme: 'A psychologically plausible novel and haunting modern day fable,' according to a critic in *The Observer.*

Süskind's style has been compared to that of another great German novelist, Kafka, for its 'bleak depiction of vulnerability' and the way he manages to create an atmosphere of fear from what is normally something trivial. *The Pigeon* has been adapted as a play and was performed in 1993 at the BAC Theatre in London. His other play, *Double Bass*, one of the most performed in Germany, has also had performances in Britain, at the Edinburgh Festival and at the National Theatre.

His most recent publication is the novella, *The Story of Mr. Summer* (1992), for which he was called 'a master of the deceptively simple tale' (*The Times*). Patrick Süskind now lives in Munich. Of *The Pigeon*:

'Süskind once again shows his outstanding gift for unravelling the implications behind very small oddities and exposing the dangerous anarchy which lurks beneath everyday events.'

The Sunday Times

JONATHAN SWIFT (1667-1745)

Anglo-Irish satirist and poet

Born in Dublin to English parents, Swift was educated at Kilkenny Grammar School (Congreve was a fellow pupil) and then Trinity College, Dublin. In 1689, through a family connection, he went to work as secretary to the statesman and writer, Sir William Temple. It was in Temple's splendid library that Swift developed into a scholar and poet. He returned to Ireland in 1695 to take holy orders but then returned to work for Temple. Here he met Esther Johnson, the young daughter of a servant, whom he called 'Stella'.

When Sir William died in 1699, Swift found he was 'unprovided both of friend and living'. He returned to Ireland where his old college made him Doctor of Divinity. Stella and her companion joined him. During Queen Anne's reign (1702-14), he divided his time between Ireland and England, becoming an active member of London's literary and political scene. Through Congreve, whom he had met at school, he made friends with Whig supporters Addison and Steele and contributed articles to their journals, *The Tatler* and *The Spectator*. He also published the first of his important satires, *The Battle of the Books* (1704), which defends ancient against modern literature. Also in 1704 he published *A Tale of a Tub*, a satire on 'corruption of religion and learning' and against religious extremism. He also wrote a series of pamphlets on church matters, *Argument against Abolishing Christianity* (1708) being considered one of the best. These satires gave him notoriety and established him as a wit.

He changed his political allegiance to the Tory party in 1710, and supported the party with pamphlets such as *The Conduct of the Allies* (1711), supporting the peace proposed in the Continental campaign. He also accepted editorship of the Tory journal, *The Examiner* (1710-11). As he moved in literary circles, he met other Tory supporters - such as Gay and Pope - with whom he formed the Scriblerus Club.

Their aim was to satirise 'false taste'. In 1710 he began his *Journal to Stella*, a series of affectionate epistles to his young friend. This was published posthumously.

The collapse of the Tory Government on Queen Anne's death saw Swift depart to Ireland to become Dean of St. Patrick's Cathedral in Dublin. Now he concentrated on Irish affairs. Although he claims to have had no love for Ireland, he was a conscientious Dean and did much to champion causes on behalf of the people, becoming a leading patriot. Many eloquent pamphlets were written on Irish oppression, among them *Drapiers Letters* in 1724 which prevented a debased coinage from being introduced.

Returning to London in 1726, he published one of the greatest satirical works, *Gulliver's Travels*, with the intention 'to vex the world rather than divert it'. Using a parody of the travel tale, like Defoe's *Robinson Crusoe*, his undaunted hero moves through the four fantasy lands of Lilliput, Brobdingnag, Laputa and Houyhnhnmland, their alternative societies providing means of social satire by making comparisons with what Swift saw as the foolishness of his own. It differs from his other satires in being masked by the fairy tale element. It has become a popular children's story - but only usually the first book and with the satire edited out.

In 1728 Stella died and Swift was grief stricken. Several pamphlets suggesting how the people of Ireland might improve their situation were ignored. In 1729 Swift published *A Modest Proposal*, a grim attack on the Irish people, suggesting they make practical and economical use of their children by fattening them to feed the rich; they lived like beasts so like beasts they should be treated. Many were shocked and thought him insane, missing the irony of the piece.

During his last years in Ireland, Swift wrote some of his best poems, including *Verses on the Death of Dr. Swift* (1731), mixing pathos and humour. In 1742 he was declared insane (though it is now known he was suffering the advanced stages of Meunières disease) and became a bitter recluse. He died in 1745 leaving money to found a hospital for imbeciles. The people of Ireland mourned him and, buried beside Stella in St. Patrick's Cathedral, he had written his own epitaph (in Latin) which describes him as being 'where fierce (or savage) indignation can no longer tear his heart'.

Swift was a prolific and versatile writer of political pamphlets, those relating to Irish affairs and church matters, and miscellaneous verses as well as the prose satires for which he is famous. Nearly all were published anonymously and without payment - he only received payment for *Gulliver's Travels*. His works are original, imaginative and show a great deal of reasoning in his opposition against injustices. Yet he alienated many writers, including Dr. Johnson and Thackeray, who found him too bitter, negative and misanthropic. In the eighteenth and nineteenth centuries he was undervalued as a writer but in the twentieth century his reputation has been revised, with more biographical information attaching importance to his devotion to friends, charity towards ordinary people and championship of common sense.

DONNA TARTT (born 1964)

American novelist

Born in Mississippi, USA and educated at the University of Mississippi and Bennington College, New York City.

She was a precocious child and began writing poetry as early as five. Her first novel, *The Secret History* (1992) was given much pre-publication hype by the media, including a profile in *Vanity Fair* and reports of the rights being sold for lucrative foreign and film rights. It more than justified its publicity for, despite having taken eight years to write, *The Secret History* met with overwhelming popular and critical success.

It was written while Tartt was a student at Bennington College. She uses this, loosely, as the setting for what appears to be a campus murder mystery. It marks an astonishing debut, not merely for the clever juggling of the plot and gift for black humour, but for the original way it combines the erudite with suspense: 'a thinking person's thriller', *Newsday* called it. Praise was universal, though the appeal tended to be more to women than men. Those few critics who did not like it found it too long and the literary allusions too pretentious. One critic in favour said, 'it reads like Barbara Vine's *A Fatal Inversion* rewritten by Scott Fitzgerald.' Barbara Vine herself (the distinguished crime writer Ruth Rendell) confessed, 'As a murder mystery it is one of the best I have ever read. But as a first novel it takes my breath away it is so accomplished.' The *New York Times* found Donna Tartt's first novel 'forceful, cerebral and impeccably controlled .... Ferociously well-paced .... a remarkably powerful novel.'

LEO TOLSTOY (1828-1910)

Russian novelist, short story writer, playwright and philosopher

Born into the Russian aristocracy at the family estate of Yasnaya Polyana in central Russia, Tolstoy lost both parents when still a child. Brought up by a series of aunts, his education was erratic. Although he went to Kazan University in 1844 to study law, his youth was spent more in bordellos than in high society, which he shunned. In 1847 he inherited the family estate and title, his father having died in 1837, but did little to reform his dissipated life, though he had periodic moments of moral and spiritual crisis.

He joined the army in 1851, on his brother Nikolai's invitation, and served in the Crimean War. The experience had a profound effect on him, prompting him to write the strongly anti-war, *Sevastopol Sketches* (1855-6) and *The Cossacks* (1863). After the war he travelled widely in Europe, including England. In 1852, still a young man in his early twenties, he published his first written work, the first book of a remarkable autobiographical trilogy, *Childhood* based on his early life. *Boyhood* (1854) and *Youth* (1857) followed later. In 1857 he showed the first outward sign of moving away from his family traditions by setting up a school for peasants' children on his estate. He also began an affair with a peasant woman. In 1859 he published *Family Happiness*.

His brother Nikolai died of tuberculosis in 1860. In 1862, after a whirlwind romance, he married Sofya Bers and settled on his estate, though domestic life was far from calm. Shortly after his marriage he began working on his masterpiece, the grand epic novel *War and Peace*. From 1863-9 he chronicled the fortunes of three aristocratic families during the years leading to Napoleon's invasion of Russia in 1812. He created memorable characters, among them Pierre Bezukhov, the confused idealist, a self-portrait, representing Tolstoy's spiritual and moral conflict.

Another great work was begun in 1873 with *Anna Karenina*, the first part of which was published in 1875, the second in 1877. Set against the backdrop of the high society that he himself shunned, it is a compelling and tragic story of an adulterous love affair. Not only is it considered one of the greatest novels, but its high drama has led to several film and television adaptations.

In the 1880s Tolstoy became much concerned with religious and moral questions. He attempted to record his philosophies on life in such works as *A Confession* (1879-82), *What Men Live By* (1882), *What I Believe* (1883) and *What Is Art?* (1898). He had become disillusioned by worldliness and had begun to turn from the church to form his own style of religion. This incorporated pacifism, self-abrogation, the abolition of governments and churches and a belief that God was to be found within man. He began living as he preached, giving away his wealth, freeing the serfs, living an austere life by abstaining from meat, alcohol, smoking and even sex, moving to a cottage on the edge of his former estate to live as a peasant.

His later written works show a change in his thinking. They include *The Death of Ivan Ilyich* (1886), *The Kreutzer*

Sonata (1889), *Master and Man* (1895), *Resurrection* (1899) and *Hadji Murad* (1904). Many were influenced by his beliefs and Yasnaya Polyana became a place of pilgrimage for those who saw Tolstoy as a spiritual leader. His pacifist creed of 'resist not evil' gained many disciples, including Ghandi, and writers who were influenced by him and helped establish his reputation in England include George Bernard Shaw, E.M. Forster and D.H. Lawrence.

However, there were many critics, not least the Russian Orthodox Church who, in 1901, excommunicated him and banned many of his works. A rift was caused in the family, with Tolstoy's thirteen children being divided between their parents. Constant quarrels with Sofya made life unbearable. He died at the railway station in Astapovo, attempting to leave home. A large number of his works were translated in his lifetime, including the *Collected Works* (translated 1899-1902).

'Leo Tolstoy was torn by violent contradictions. A wealthy aristocrat, he tried to give up his possessions; passionately sensual, he desired to renounce all sensual pleasures'. Such conflicts within the man himself led to a deep human understanding for the complexities and conflicting emotions of his characters. What made him so great a writer is not so much the vastness of scale, the great 'sprawl' of life as it has been called, but his ability to enter into the situation of each of his characters - to feel for them and invite the reader to do the same.

VINCENT VAN GOGH (1853-90)

Dutch painter

Born in Zundert, the son of a Dutch pastor, he originally studied theology and was a lay preacher before taking up painting in 1880. He also worked for a time as a school master in England before studying under van Mauve at the Antwerp Academy. His work remained thoroughly unacademic in its realist subject matter and bold expressionistic style - *The Potato Eaters* (1885) is an example of this.

He moved to Paris in 1886. Here his work was variously influenced by Degas, Gauguin and Seurat, although without compromising his enigmatic use of colour and powerful impasto brushwork. When van Gogh moved to Arles in Provence, Gauguin joined him there in 1888. After a quarrel, van Gogh cut off part of his own earlobe and in 1889 he entered an asylum at St Remy. The following year he committed suicide.

Some of his revealing letters have been translated (*The Letters of Vincent van Gogh to His Brother, 1927*). The Arles paintings vividly testify to his intense emotional involvement in his art; among the best known are *The Yellow Chair* and several *Sunflowers* (1888) which are in the National Gallery, London.

One of the leaders of the Post-Impressionist painters, van Gogh executed still life and landscape paintings, one of the best known being *A Cornfield with Cypresses* (1889). His importance in the establishment of a new direction to Expressionist and Abstract art is enormous, and his work had a resonant and continuing influence on twentieth century art worldwide. Ironically, he did not sell a single painting during his lifetime.

DEREK WALCOTT (born 1930)

West Indian poet and dramatist

Derek Walcott was born in the Castries, St. Lucia. His father died when he was young and, influenced by his mother's fondness for verse (she was a teacher) and the Methodist hymn singing of his church, he started writing poetry as a child.

He was educated at St. Mary's College, Castries and University College of the West Indies, Jamaica. Afterwards he taught in various schools in the Caribbean. He moved into journalism as a feature writer and drama critic on West

Indian newspapers and in 1950 founded the St. Lucia Arts Guild. He now divides his time between the Caribbean and the USA where, since 1985, he has been visiting Professor of Poetry at Boston University.

His first volume of poetry, *25 Poems* (1984), was published when he was only eighteen but it was not until *In a Green Night: Poems 1948-60* (1962) that he gained widespread recognition. This was consolidated by *The Castaway* (1965) and *The Gulf* (1970) and an impressive autobiographical poem, *Another Life* (1973).

Subsequent volumes of poetry include *Sea Grapes* (1976), *The Star-Apple Kingdom* (1980), *The Fortunate Traveller* (1981), *Midsummer* (1983), *Collected Poems* (1986) and *The Arkansas Testament* (1987). His most ambitious work, *Omeros*, was published in 1990. This is a reworking of the themes of *The Iliad* and *The Odyssey* in a Caribbean setting.

Derek Walcott was the founder director of the Little Carib Theatre Workshop which later became the Trinidad Theatre Workshop (1959-71) and has written numerous plays which received their first performances there. Among his best are *Dream Monkey Mountain* (1971, originally commissioned by RSC), *The Joker of Seville* (1978) and *O Babylon!* (1978) set amongst the Rastafarian community. This was performed in London at the Riverside Studios in 1976.

Walcott has received numerous literary awards both in America and Britain, among them the Guinness Award (1961), The Heinman Award, The Eugene O'Neill Foundation Fellowship and The Queen's Gold Medal for Poetry (1988). He received the OBE in 1972 and the Nobel Prize in 1992. Much of what Derek Walcott writes is autobiographical and is concerned with a search for identity and roots. This often involves conflict of race (Walcott is English speaking with two English grandparents). He asks in an early poem how he is to choose 'between this Africa and the English tongue I love?' He is also concerned with conflicts of culture and of religion: he was brought up as an Anglicised Methodist in a French speaking Catholic Voodoo culture. The contrasting influences of Caribbean and European culture, 'the choice of home or exile, self-realisation or spiritual betrayal of one's country' exercises him greatly. Many poems explore both sides of such conflicts but after *The Castaway* this conflict is seen to distance him from his community. Other central concerns are with political tyranny and racism evident in *A Far Cry from Africa*. In this, the Mau Mau revolt makes him reconsider his allegiance to Kenya.

The plays, like the poems, are concerned with national identity and involve singing, storytelling, dance, Creole vocabulary and rich metaphor and Calypso rhythms. In a mixture of realism and fantasy they draw on a wide variety of theatrical traditions. *The Odyssey*, performed by the RSC in 1992, is rich in classical allusion but has Caribbean and European influences as well, and deals with sufferings of exile. Derek Walcott's poetry and drama are very much related. His concern for West Indian heritage and literature have not only made him a leading writer from the Caribbean but also a prominent contemporary writer in the West.

EVELYN WAUGH (1903-1966)

British novelist

Born in Hampstead, London, the son of publisher, Arthur Waugh. Educated at Lancing and Hertford College, Oxford. He studied art and taught in private schools. For a time he worked for *The Daily Express*. He mixed with high society. Here he found the principal objects of his satire in the early novels, the frivolous generation of 'bright young things' of post-war Britain, although the range of his contempt was vast.

His first novel, *Decline and Fall* (1928), based on his own teaching experience, focuses on public schools. This and *Vile Bodies* (1930) established his reputation, almost immediately, as a leading satirical novelist. He worked for a time as a foreign correspondent: novels such as *Scoop* (1938), a satire on journalism, and *Black Mischief* (1932), on tyranny in an African state, explore with comic consequences the clash between civilisation and barbarism. This theme is used in an English setting in *A Handful of Dust* (1934), a tragicomedy of adultery. *The Loved One* (1948) satirises the Hollywood commercialism of death.

His comedy, always black, became much darker after his conversion to Roman Catholicism in 1930 and his satire grew less frivolous, with a sharper edge. Because of his change of faith, his first marriage was not annulled until 1936. A year later he married Laura Herbert and they had six children. During World War II he served with the Royal Marines. *Put Out More Flags* (1942) was written during this period and he took leave to write what was to become his best known novel, *Brideshead Revisited* (1945). This marked a change from a satirical to a more serious tone, bringing up issues such as tradition and religion. An enormously successful television adaptation made in 1980 and scripted by John Mortimer saw the popularity of this novel soar.

An historical novel set in Rome, *Helena* (1950), was Waugh's favourite, though not popular. *Men at Arms* (1952), *Officers and Gentlemen* (1955) and *Unconditional Surrender* (1961) form the trilogy, *Sword of Honour* (published together in 1965), and describe Waugh's army experiences. The trilogy became highly successful and was dramatised on both TV and radio. Later books include *The Ordeal of Gilbert Pinfold* (1957), a penetrating self-portrait of an alcoholic author succumbing to the effects of a breakdown.

Many of Waugh's novels have a naïve central character and blend farce and tragedy. He makes rich use of language and his style is urbane. Other novels include *Scott King's Modern Europe* (1947), *Tactical Exercise* (1954) and *Basil Seal Rides Again* (1963). His other work consists of story collections such as *Mr. Loveday's Little Outing* (1936) and many travel books based on experiences in the Mediterranean, Africa and South America, selections from which are collected under the title, *When the Going was Good* (1946). His last travel book was *A Tourist in Africa*

(1960). He wrote biographies of the nineteenth century poet and painter Rossetti (1926), the Jesuit martyr Edmund Campian (1935) and his friend Ronald Knox (1959). *A Little Learning*, the first volume of his autobiography, was published in 1964. The posthumous publication of his *Journals* (1976) and *Letters* (1980) added to his stature as a great comic observer.

Waugh spent his later years in Somerset with his family, living and dressing like a cantankerous country squire. He has founded a literary dynasty. Among his children are Auberon Waugh, the editor, columnist and novelist and Margaret Fitzherbert the biographer. Several of his grandchildren have also become writers, the best-known being novelist Daisy Waugh.

EDITH WHARTON (1862-1937)

American novelist

Born Edith Newbold Jones on 24 January 1862 in New York, during the American Civil War. The only daughter of wealthy and distinguished parents, she enjoyed a privileged childhood. She was educated privately in the United States and abroad. In 1885 she married Edward Robbins Wharton, a close friend of one of her two elder brothers. The couple travelled, and Edith made new literary acquaintances and devoted her time to writing and decorating the various houses in which they lived. During this time she suffered from depression, intense fatigue and hysteria. However, she gradually recovered and, in 1903, Edith and her husband began a long period of travel in England and Europe, meeting Henry James and other literary and artistic people. The marriage was not a success and the couple separated in 1911. From 1907 until her death, Edith made her home in France. Her war work with refugees and orphans won her the Legion d'Honneur in 1916.

During her life she published more than forty volumes: novels, stories, verse, essays, travel books and memoirs.

Her literary career began with the publication of poems and stories in *Scribner's Magazine.* Her first volume of short stories, *The Greater Inclination* (1899), was followed by a novella, *The Touchstone* (1900). It was *The House of Mirth* (1905), which established her as a leading novelist. Many other works followed, including *Madame de Treymes* (1907), *Ethan Frome* (1911), *The Reef* (1912), *The Custom of the Country* (1913), *The Age of Innocence* (1920 and awarded the Pulitzer Prize in 1921), *The Mother's Recompense* (1925), *Hudson River Bracketed* (1929) and the autobiography, *A Backward Glance* (1934). The last unfinished novel, *The Buccaneers,* was published posthumously a year after she died in 1937 at her home in Paris, aged 75 years.

RICHARD WILBUR (born 1921)

American poet

Born in New York City, his father was the artist L Wilbur. He was educated at Amherst College and Harvard, returning there to teach after serving in the US Army during World War II. He subsequently held teaching posts at Wellesley and Wesleyan Universities. He was writer-in-residence at Smith College during the 1970s.

He began his career as a poet with *The Beautiful Changes* (1947), written in response to the war and its effects. He won the Harriet Monroe Memorial Prize in 1948. A second collection of poetry followed, *Ceremony and Other Poems* (1950). This, like the first book, touched on themes of personal and public dislocation. Subsequent volumes have been *A Bestiary* (1955), *The Things of this World* (1956 - winner of both a Pulitzer Prize and The National Book Award), *Poems 1943-56* (1957), *Advice to a Prophet and Other Poems* (1961), *The Poems of Richard Wilbur* (1963), *Complaint* (1968), *Walking to Sleep - New Poems and Translations* (1969), *Seed Leaves* (1974), *The Mind Reader* (1976), *Seven Poems* (1981), *Verses on the*

Times (1981) and *New and Collected Poems* (1988). The latter won him another Pulitzer Prize.

He is a distinguished translator of poetry and drama, notably Moliere's plays, *The Misanthrope* (1955), *Tartuffe* (1963) and *The School for Wives* (1971). He has also made a verse translation of Racine's *Andromache* (1982) and collaborated with Lillian Hellman on the lyrics for Leonard Bernstein's comic opera, *Candide* (1957). In 1963 he received the Bollingen Prize for translation. *The Whale and Other Uncollected Translations* appeared in 1982.

He has also published verse for children in *Loudmouse* (1963) and *Opposites* (1973) and a collection of literary essays in *Responses: Prose Pieces 1953-76* (1976). *On My Own Work* (1983) is an exercise in self-criticism. Richard Wilbur's poetry is elegant, formal, witty and urbane. He believes in order, as his use of language and detailed images shows. His was not the then-fashionable style of 'confessional' poetry such as his contemporaries Robert Lowell and James Dickey were writing. Rather, Wilbur's work was more detached and academic and, according to some of his critics, lacking in passion. Randall Jarrell commented, 'Mr. Wilbur never goes too far but he never goes far enough'.

Richard Wilbur has written:

'Poems ... are not addressed to anybody in particular ... they are conflicts with disorder, not messages from one person to another.'

'It is the province of poets to make some order in the world ... but people can't afford to forget that there is a reality in things which survive all order, great and small.'

'If my poems are unfashionable towards nature I must blame this warp on a rural, pleasant and somewhat solitary childhood.'

OSCAR WILDE (1854-1900)

Irish playwright, novelist, essayist, poet and wit

Born in Dublin, the son of a distinguished surgeon. His mother was a literary hostess and wrote poetry and passionate nationalistic articles under the pen-name, 'Speranza'. She was a great influence on his life and he worshipped her. He was educated at Trinity College, Dublin and later at Magdalen College, Oxford (1874-8). Here he excelled in classics gaining a double first and winning the Newdigate Prize. He also became a conspicuous member of the Aesthetic Movement, putting their doctrine of 'Art for Art's Sake' into practise by his flamboyant style of dress and decadent life style.

Despite his wit and charm, which captivated many, reception was hostile from the more traditional members of Victorian society. He was satirised in *Punch* and, as 'Bunthorne', by Gilbert and Sullivan in their comic opera, *Patience*. Wilde benefited from the publicity when the D'Oyly Carte Company took the production to America. He went too, embarking on a lecture tour that would explain English aestheticism to the Americans. This proved highly successful and his personal appearances made him a lot of money - the Americans at first bewildered, then enchanted, by the witty young man with flowing hair, velvet breeches and silk stockings.

In 1884 he married Constance Lloyd, whom he had met in Dublin. They lived in Chelsea and Wilde proceeded to turn his home into 'The House Beautiful', subject of one of his lectures. The marriage seemed happy and they had two sons, Cyril and Vyvyan. In order to provide the means for his extravagant lifestyle, Wilde embarked on another lecture tour and for a time wrote book reviews for the *Pall Mall Gazette*, later becoming editor of *The Women's World*.

His reputation as a writer rests with the work he produced during a seven year period beginning in 1888 when *The*

Happy Prince and Other Stories, written for his sons, was published. His prose style, made more lucid and concise by book reviewing, produced stories that were simple and direct with a moral message. He followed these with two other collections of stories, *The House of Pomegranates* (1891) and *Lord Arthur Saville's Crimes and other Stories* (1891). He also wrote a number of social essays, among them *The Critic as Artist* (1891) and *The Soul of Man under Socialism* (1891), a plea for individual and artistic freedom.

The Picture of Dorian Gray was also published in this year and is Wilde's only novel. His story of a young man corrupted by a decadent life aroused scandal. Wilde defended the book by writing in the preface that, 'there is no such thing as a moral or immoral book. Books are well written or badly written. That is all.'

Wilde is best remembered for his plays. These scintillating social comedies replaced the stereotypes of Victorian melodrama with characters drawn from the very society that flocked to see them. Through witty dialogue, Wilde satirised Victorian society for its attitudes and hypocrisy and became the most important dramatist of the age. These four plays, *Lady Windermere's Fan* (1892), *A Woman of No Importance* (1893), *An Ideal Husband* (1895), and his masterpiece, *The Importance of Being Earnest* (1895), enjoyed West End success then as they still do to this day.

Another play, the exotic *Salome* (1891), was written in French and translated into English by Lord Alfred Douglas, son of the Marquis of Queensberry. Wilde first met 'Bosie' Douglas at Oxford in 1891, when he helped him escape from a blackmail attempt. Wilde felt a great attraction to Bosie, who was to prove mean, vindictive and possessive. Wilde was later to call him a 'gilded pillar of infamy', though their bond was deep. Bosie Douglas was to be Wilde's downfall. Queensberry took exception to his son's friendship with Wilde and, himself a man of violent and excessive temper, caused many scenes in public places. He finally left a card at Wilde's club on which he had written, 'To Oscar Wilde -

posing as a sodomite'. This was so public an accusation that Wilde knew he had either to accept the public vilification or defend himself.

Wilde had broken so many taboos in Victorian society - and become so successful - that he believed himself unassailable. He took action for libel against Queensberry, but the prosecution produced sufficient evidence of Wilde's liaisons with male servants and other lower-class homosexuals, that Wilde was himself sent to trial and subsequently convicted for homosexual practices. He was sentenced to two years hard labour at Pentonville and Reading gaols (1895-97). The experience broke Wilde's health and his spirit. In 1897, from prison, he wrote *De Profundis* (From the Depths), a long and bitter letter to Lord Alfred Douglas reproaching him for causing his downfall and providing an apologia for his own conduct, claiming he stood 'in symbolic relations to the art and culture' of his age. It was published in part in 1905 and in its entirety in 1962. It is very personal and moving and contains some of his finest prose. George Bernard Shaw said that, 'there was more laughter between the lines of that book than in a thousand farces by men of no genius'.

On his release from prison, Wilde left for France to live in exile. He described himself as, 'broken hearted, ruined, disgraced, a leper and a pariah to men'. He called himself 'Sebastian Melmoth' - Sebastian suggested by the arrows of his convict garb; *Melmoth the Wanderer* was a Gothic novel by Maturin from whom Wilde was a descendant. While in exile in France, he wrote *The Ballad of Reading Gaol* (1898), his last and finest poem based on his own experiences. He spent his last years impoverished and lonely. His wife had divorced him and died in 1898. He was forbidden to see his sons, and Bosie Douglas and he had parted over an argument about money. Dejected and crippled by illness, he died in Paris aged 46.

Wilde once told a friend, 'I have put my genius into my life, only my talent into my works'. In life he was certainly a brilliant raconteur, witty conversationalist, master of the epigram and natural performer but the 'talent' he put into his written work - the plays, poems, novel, essays and short stories - was immense and shows him to be one of the most gifted and most quoted Victorian writers. His friend Richard le Galliene said, 'He made dying Victorianism laugh at itself, and what serious reformers had laboured for years to accomplish, he did in a moment with the flash of an epigram; gaily with humour and wit for his weapons.' Though a brilliant social satirist of Victorian hypocrisy, it was not enough to save him when he contravened their moral code. 'Somehow or other, I'll be famous, and if not famous, I'll be notorious' unwittingly declared the young Oscar Wilde. He proved to be both.

P.G. (PELHAM GRENVILLE) WODEHOUSE (1881-1975)

British novelist and short story writer

Born in Guildford in 1881, he was the son of a civil servant who became a judge in Hong Kong. Wodehouse was brought up by various aunts and was educated at Dulwich College. After working for the Hong Kong and Shanghai Bank for two years, he turned to journalism, writing the 'By the Way' column in the *Globe*. He also contributed a series of school stories for a boys magazine, the *Captain* in one of which Psmith made his first appearance. He later published extensively in the *Strand Magazine* and *Punch*.

After 1909 Wodehouse lived mainly abroad, eventually settling in the USA, where his talent blossomed. Known to his friends as 'Plum', he wrote many lyrics for musicals in collaboration with composers such as Jerome Kern, Gershwin and Irving Berlin. However, it was his humorous novels that made him into a cult figure. The tales of Bertie Wooster and his manservant, Jeeves, Psmith, the members of the Drones Club, Lord Emsworth and his prize sow, the Empress of Blandings, made Wodehouse's books international best-sellers.

In 1940 Wodehouse was captured in Le Touquet and interned by the Nazis. He was released after a short time but not allowed to leave Germany. He unwisely accepted an invitation to broadcast to America from Berlin, which led to accusations that he was pro-Nazi. Both Evelyn Waugh and George Orwell wrote spirited defences of him, effectively disproving the treason charges. He went to Paris after the war and then returned to the United States where he continued with his writing. He became an American citizen in 1955.

Wodehouse wrote over one hundred and twenty volumes and his work has won world-wide acclaim, translated into many languages. A few weeks before his death he was created a Knight of the British Empire in the New Year's Honours list of 1975. He died on St. Valentine's Day at the age of ninety-three. *The Times* hailed him as 'a comic genius recognised in his lifetime as a classic and an old master of farce.'

The Man with Two Left Feet and *Uneasy Money* appeared in 1917, followed by *Piccadilly Jim* (1918), *A Damsel in Distress* (1919), *The Indiscretions of Archie* (1921), *The Clicking of Cuthbert* (1922), *My Man Jeeves* (1919), *The Inimitable Jeeves* (1923), *Carry On Jeeves* (1925) and *Uncle Fred in the Springtime* (1939). His autobiography appeared in three volumes: *Performing Flea* (1953), *Over Seventy* (1957) and *Aunts Aren't Gentlemen* (1974).

WILLIAM WORDSWORTH (1770-1850)

British poet

Born in Cockermouth, Cumberland. His father was a lawyer but both parents died when he was young and he was brought up by relatives. He was educated at Hawkshead School and at St. John's College, Cambridge. In 1790 he took a walking holiday to France, the Alps and Italy, and returned to France late in 1791 to spend a year there. During this period he was inspired by a passionate belief in the French Revolution and republican ideals.

He fell in love with the daughter of a surgeon, Annette Vallon, who bore him an illegitimate daughter (this secret was unknown until the 1920s). Forced back to England by the threat of war and financial pressure, he published *An Evening Walk* (1793) and *Descriptive Sketches* (1793) but, disillusioned with the violence of the French Revolution, the years 1793-5 were a period of deep unhappiness and uncertainty.

A legacy in 1795 changed his fortune, enabling him to pursue a career as a poet and to set up home with his sister, Dorothy, who became his devoted companion. She lived with him for the rest of his life. Her journals recorded their shared memories and Wordsworth drew upon them for his poetry, as in his famous poem, *Daffodils*. They moved to Dorset where he wrote a blank verse tragedy, *The Borderers*, and then to Somerset, to be near their friend and neighbour, Coleridge. The three formed a close friendship. Coleridge called Wordsworth, 'a very great man, the only man to whom at all times .... I feel myself inferior.' He said that they were 'three people with one soul'.

In 1798 the two poets published *Lyrical Ballads*. This marked a turning point in English poetry and the beginning of Romanticism. Wordsworth's aim was 'to choose incidents and situations from common life' describing them, 'in a selection of language really used by men'. Wordsworth contributed more than half of the poems, among them *Lines Written Above Tintern Abbey* (1798). This was inspired by a visit to the ruined Abbey in South Wales, five years after he had first been there. The book's novel language and subject matter were appreciated by only a small section of readers at first. It was added to and republished several times.

The trio visited Germany in 1798-9 where the 'Lucy' poems were written. On returning, William and Dorothy moved to Dove Cottage in Grasmere in the Lake District. Here they stayed for a number of years and Wordsworth wrote or started to write many of his greatest works. These include *Michael*, *The Prelude* (his greatest single poem, in which he records his childhood, its joys and terrors, and his development as a poet), *Sonnets Dedicated to Liberty* and a great part of *The Recluse* (later called *The Excursion*). He wrote many of the poems that were to be included in the second edition of *Lyrical Ballads* (1800) as well as the new preface, a manifesto for Romanticism which caused controversy. In 1802 he married his friend from childhood, Mary Hutchinson. They subsequently had five children. Also in that year he composed *Revolution and Independence* and parts of his ode, *Intimations of Immortality from Recollections of Early Childhood*, both of which appeared in *Poems in Two Volumes* (1807). Later major works include *Ode to Duty*, *Miscellaneous Sonnets* and *Sonnets Dedicated to Liberty*.

In 1810 he had a famous quarrel with Coleridge over the latter's drunken behaviour. Their relationship was never the same again. Saddened by this, and grief stricken two years later when two of his children died, Wordsworth moved from Dove Cottage to Rydal Mount where he lived until he died. He also took on the lucrative post of Distributor of Stamps for Westmorland. *The Excursion* was finally published in 1814 and the following year *The White Doe of Rylstone* (1815) and *Poems, Including Lyrical Ballads* (1815) were published.

The change in Wordsworth in his mature years attracted criticism, particularly from his younger contemporaries. The early revolutionary had turned into a staunch conservative, working for the Government and campaigning for the local Tory candidate. His later poetry is generally considered to be inferior. Wordsworth once found nature an unfailing source of 'joy and passion' and he was able to transfer this into words. Now it was 'dull', according to Byron and Shelley, and Robert Browning called him 'The Lost Leader'. The later Wordsworth sought more to rationalise and moralise upon earlier feelings, the 'romantic' contacts with nature becoming more spiritual. *Peter Bell*, a tale in verse, and *The Waggoner* were published in 1819. Much of his later inspiration came from his travels to Scotland and the Continent. Already a pillar of the establishment and the most famous of poets, Wordsworth succeeded his friend Southey as Poet Laureate in 1843.

Thomas de Quincy, author of *Recollections of the Lake Poets* (1834-39), wrote, 'up to 1820 the name of Wordsworth was trampled underfoot; from 1820-1830 it was militant; from 1830-1835 it has been triumphant'. Wordsworth died in 1850. A few months later, Mary Wordsworth published *The Prelude* posthumously and his *Poetical and Prose Works* appeared in 1896, as did Dorothy Wordsworth's *Journals*.

Wordsworth and Coleridge, together with Southey, were known as 'The Lake Poets', because that beautiful part of the North-West is where they lived and drew much of their inspiration. Dorothy Wordsworth wrote in her journals that it was, 'a place made for all kinds of beautiful works of art and literature'. It drew tourists even then and Wordsworth's own *Guide to the Lakes* (1822) was a best-seller in its day. It is the mark of his stature in English Literature that today Dove Cottage, Rydal Mount and the surrounding countryside have become places of literary pilgrimage for people from all over the world.

W. B. (William Butler) YEATS (1865-1939)

Irish poet, critic and playwright

Born near Dublin to a cultured Irish Protestant family (his father was a painter), he was educated at the Godolphin School in London and later at the High School and School of Art in Dublin. He had spent much of his boyhood in his mother's home county of Sligo, absorbing the beauty of the countryside and the wealth of Irish myths and legends that were to feature in his early work. He wrote prolifically - poetry, prose and plays.

Yeats' poetry falls into three main periods. Firstly, the poetry of what is often described as 'The Celtic Twilight' period (he wrote *The Celtic Twilight*, a collection of Irish folk tales, in 1893). As a young man, Yeats had been a leading member of the Aesthetic Movement which, much influenced by the romanticism of the Pre-Raphaelites, had spurned Victorian materialism. Instead, they turned to mysticism in order to achieve spiritual fulfilment. Yeats had always had an interest in folklore and began his literary career by drawing upon and reviving Irish legends, 'the land of the faery'. The poetry of this period has dream-like qualities and a simple melodic beauty. To this early period belong *The Wanderings of Oisin* (1889), *The Countess Cathleen and other Legends and Lyrics* (1892 - a poetic play), *The Wind Among the Reeds* (1899) and *The Shadowy Waters* (1900). During this period he became interested in the Irish Republican Movement, meeting John O'Leary and the beautiful revolutionary Maud Gonne, who was the subject of much of the early love poetry. He also met Lady Gregory, a leading figure of the Irish Revival movement at this time. With her he was later to found the Abbey Theatre.

In 1892 Yeats formed the Irish Literary Society in London and Dublin. Between 1900-10 Yeats concentrated more upon drama and philosophical writings. The poetry from the turn of the century shows a change of style. He moved away from the romantic and nostalgic towards more public and political themes. The language is more colloquial and the use of dramatic speech is frequent. Influenced by Ezra Pound and T.S. Eliot, both of whom he had met in London, his poetry became more austere: *The Green Helmet* (1910), *Responsibilities* (1914), *The Wild Swans at Coole* (1917), *The Second Coming* and one of his most famous poems, *Easter* (1916). All these were included in *Michael Robartes and the Dancer* (1921), in which, once despairing, Yeats is seen to renew his faith in heroic patriotism.

From 1922-1928 Yeats was elected to the Senate of the Irish Free State but after a public career he turned from politics to mysticism and philosophy and devoted his last years to writing. This last period contains some of his greatest, as well as most obscure, poetry. In 1917 he had bought Thoor Ballybee, a derelict stone tower near Coole Park, County Galway, and used it as a symbol in many of his poems. *The Tower* (1928) which includes *Sailing to Byzantium, Leda and the Swan* and *Among School Children* is considered to be the peak of his poetic achievement. It shows a rich lyricism and deals with contradictions between art and politics. He had by this time developed a system of symbols, referred to in his prose work, *A Vision* (1925). The poetry of this period shows increasing use of these symbols which enrich but often obscure the meaning for the reader.

These later volumes include *The Winding Stair* (1929), *The King of the Great Clock Tower* (1934) and *A Full Moon in March* (1935). *Words for Music Perhaps* contains twenty-five songs written for the puppet characters Crazy Jane, Jack the Journeyman, the Bishop, Old Tom and God, set in a world of dreams, rhymes and riddles. In these, Yeats' philosophy hides behind the mask of child-like simplicity. He said of his later poetry that every poem he wrote had been haunted by spectres of 'lust and rage'. This begins with *Parnell's Funeral and other Poems* (1935) and feelings of anger and resentment against the cruelty and chaos of the period dominate *News Poems* (1938) and the posthumous *Last Poems and Two Plays* (1939).

Yeats' prose shares many qualities of the poems. It is simple and lucid, with richly visual phrases and it has a rhythmical charm. He wrote critical and literary essays, collected in *The Cutting of an Agate* (1912), *Ideas of Good and Evil* (1903) and *Discoveries* (1906). In these, he sets forth his artistic and philosophical ideas. *A Vision* (1925) was reputedly dictated by spirits to his wife, the medium George Hyde-Lees whom he married in 1917 and who was influential in his work. He wrote occult stories in *Rosa Alchemica* (1897), where the magician figure, later to feature in the poems, first appears. Two short novels, *John Sherman and Dhoya* (1891) and *The Speckled Bird* (1897-1901), deal with the conflict between the poet and magician. Yeats also wrote several anthologies of Irish folklore including *Fairy and Folktales of the Irish Peasantry* (1888), *Fairy and Folk Tales* (1894), *The Celtic Twilight* (1893) and *The Secret Rose* (1897).

He edited *The Oxford Book of Modern Verse* in 1936. Volumes of autobiography appeared: *Reveries over Childhood and Youth* (1914) and *The Trembling of the Veil* (1922) followed by *Dramatis Personae* in 1935. He also edited the poetry of William Blake (1893) and of Spenser (1906).

Yeats began writing plays soon after 1890 and altogether wrote twenty. He was a strong believer in the Irish Nationalist Movement and did much to help create the Irish National Theatre. In 1904 the Abbey Theatre in Dublin was founded with Lady Gregory, whose estate at Coole was the setting for many poems. Yeats and Lady Gregory were made directors, along with J.M. Synge. Yeats' prose play *Cathleen ni Houlihan* (1902) with Maud Gonne in the title role, was one of the Abbey's earliest successes. Yeats remained director of the theatre until his death and wrote many plays for it - collected in *Plays for an Irish Theatre* (1911) and *Four Plays for Dancers* (1920). Between 1917-26 he wrote plays in the rather stylised Japanese Noh fashion. Yeats was able to find a voice for Irish causes through the theatre and his work as a playwright strengthened his skill as a poet with his use of the dramatic idioms.

Yeats was awarded the Nobel Prize for Literature in 1923 and in 1932 founded the Irish Academy of Letters. He died in the South of France in 1939 and his body was returned to Ireland in 1948. A collection of his poems was published posthumously (1950) as were a collection of his plays (1952) and major collections of his letters.

Yeats is considered to be one of the most important writers of poetry in English in the twentieth century. 'Ireland was still small enough in the early twentieth century for one man to feel its problems personally and mould great poetry out of them ... this more than anything else establishes Yeats's pre-eminence', writes George Macbeth. Many young Irish poets, looking to find a perspective on the Ulster troubles of today have looked to Yeats for inspiration.